The Battle of Tsu-shima

between the Japanese and Russian fleets,

fought on 27th May 1905

Vladimir Ivanovich Semenov

Translator: A. B. Lindsay

Originally Published in 1913

TO THE EVERLASTING MEMORY

OF THE HEROES WHO PERISHED!

"Captain Semenoff's little volume, which would well repay translation, is a remarkably graphic and luminous account of Admiral Togo's great victory, compiled from notes taken by the author during the engagement. His account is all the more interesting as he was also on the Cesarevitch *when Admiral Vitoft made his unsuccessful attempt to escape from Port Arthur on 10th August 1904.... Every word of this little volume bears the impress of reality, and enables the reader to form a vivid picture of the various phases of the battle. There is a plan showing the positions of the contending fleets from 1.20 till 7 P.M."*

—Times Literary Supplement, 17th August 1906.

Vladimir Ivanovich Semenov

TABLE OF CONTENTS

<u>TRANSLATOR'S PREFACE</u>

<u>CHAPTER I</u>

Weather on leaving Shanghai—"Order of march"—Instructions for taking order of battle—Accident to Senyavin's engines—Manoeuvres on 26th May—Spoilt by 3rd squadron—Unpreparedness of Russian fleet—A forlorn hope—Comparison between Russian and Japanese ships—Feeling on Board the Suvoroff—Togo's whereabouts—A discussion—Will he be misled?—Will the Russian fleet slip past?—Which course to follow?—Three possibilities

<u>CHAPTER II</u>

Not yet discovered—Intercepting Japanese wireless messages—Night of 26th May—Doings in the Suvoroff—The engine-room—The ward-room—Reflections and ruminations—Commander V. V. Ignatzius—His opinion—A desperate adventure—Dawn on 27th May—The Sinano Maru runs into the hospital ships—The fleet discovered—Recall of the scouts—Four Japanese ships reported—Idzumi sighted 6.45 A.M.—And later the 3rd Japanese squadron—Russian fleet takes order of battle—11.20 A.M., opens fire—A mistake—Ship's companies have dinner—The alarm—Japanese light cruisers—Russians maneuver—Orders misunderstood—Result—Japanese main force sighted—The eve of battle—Rozhdestvensky enters the conning tower

CHAPTER III

CHAPTER IV

CHAPTER V

enemy—Effect on men's spirits—Death of Commander Ignatzius—Torpedo-boats approach—Only two serviceable guns—A tour of inspection—Effect of Japanese gun fire—Their explosive—Kursel the Courlandian—Destruction of officers' quarters—Author again wounded

CHAPTER VI

4 P.M., fleets lose each other—5 P.M., Russian fleet steams northwards—Passes the Suvoroff—The Borodino leads—The Alexander heeling over—Torpedo-boats ahead!—The Buiny— Admiral to be transferred—Attempts to collect the Staff—Death of all hands below—No boats available—Difficulty of the undertaking—Rozhdestvensky put aboard—The Buiny steams off—Description of the flag-ship—The Admiral's condition— Nebogatoff in command—Sinking of the Alexander—Overtaking the fleet—Sinking of the Oslyabya—Also of the Borodino—End of the Suvoroff

COMPOSITION OF THE OPPOSING FLEETS

FOOTNOTES

TRANSLATOR'S PREFACE

The following account of the battle of Tsu-shima, fought on 27th May 1905, is a translation of the narrative of Captain Vladimir Semenoff, a Russian naval officer who was on board the flag-ship (*Knyaz Suvoroff*) during the engagement. It is of more than usual interest, as the writer had previously served in the *Cesarevitch* at Port Arthur, and had taken part in the disastrous sally from that port on 10th August 1904.

At the great battle of which he now relates his experiences, he was present in an unofficial capacity, which gave him unlimited opportunity for observation. Moreover, the fact of his being able to make a series of notes at the time (till too seriously wounded) puts an additional stamp of reality on to his already most graphic account.

It should be remembered that the Russian Baltic fleet—Russia's final and supreme appeal to the God of Battles—left Cronstadt for the Far East on 11th September 1904, and during all the long months till the following May was slowly making its way, *viâ* the Cape of Good Hope, to Japanese waters. The difficulties encountered during that prolonged voyage were enormous. The nerves of officers and men, who constantly apprehended attempts to destroy the fleet, were in a continual state of tension: news of the outside world and especially of events in the Far East was practically unobtainable: and yet officers and men, despite the additional disadvantage of having to take their ships into action after these many months at sea, fearlessly entered into an engagement which they knew meant death, and fought their ships with a self-devotion and courage which has earned for them the admiration of the world.

Admiral Togo—flying his flag on the *Mikasa*—awaited the enemy in Japanese waters. His fleet, which, since the fall of Port Arthur on 2nd January 1905, had been relieved of its blockading duties, had spent the intervening months in repairing damage and bringing itself up to the highest state of preparation in expectation of the coming of the Baltic fleet.

To a nation like ourselves, whose first line of defence is the Navy, I venture to think that these pages will give food for thought, as, besides enabling the reader to see the paralysing and awful effect of high explosives thrown on board a modern battleship in action, they supply us with a picture of what a losing engagement means to those who lose.

When first I took up the original volume I read it merely with a view to extracting information *re* fire effect, gun power, weather conditions, formations, and other factors complementary to the result of the battle. But the narrative appeared so realistic that the thought occurred to me to place the following translation before the public.

The speed maintained by the opposing fleets during the battle is shown in the diagram attached. Dates have been expressed according to the English calendar (which is thirteen days in advance of the Russian)—otherwise the writer's own words and colloquial style have, as far as possible, been faithfully adhered to, to the detriment of literary style in translating.

It may be mentioned that this narrative comes as a supplement to the very interesting account by Politovsky of the voyage of the

Baltic fleet to the Far East—recently translated by Major Godfrey and published by John Murray under the title "From Libau to Tsu-shima."

Politovsky went down in the *Suvoroff,* and his story ends with the arrival of the fleet at Shanghai on 23rd May, the date on which he posted his last letter to Russia. The following narrative commences on 25th May, as the fleet swung out of Shanghai to meet its destiny.

A. B. L.

7th November 1906.

CHAPTER I

A fresh breeze mournfully droned through the wire rigging and angrily dispersed the ragged, low-lying clouds. The troubled waters of the Yellow Sea splashed against the side of the battleship, while a thin, cold, blinding rain fell, and the raw air penetrated to one's very bones. But a group of officers still stood on the after-bridge, watching the silhouettes of the transports slowly disappearing in the rain haze.

On their masts and yard-arms signals were being flown, the last messages and final requests of those who had been our fellow-travellers on the long tedious voyage.

Why is it that at sea a friendly greeting of this kind, expressed merely by a combination of flags, touches one's heart so deeply, and speaks to it even more than salutes, cheers, or music? Why is it that until the signal has been actually hauled down every one looks at it, silently and intently, as if real words, instead of motley-coloured pieces of cloth, were fluttering in the breeze, and becoming wet with rain? Why is it that on the signal being hauled down every one turns away, quietly moving off to his duty, as if the last quiet handshake had been given, and "good-bye" had been said for ever?

"Well!—how about the weather?" said some one—to break the silence.

"Grand," answered another with a smile. "If we get this all the way to Vladivostok, then thank the Lord! why, a general battle will be impossible."

Once more a signal was made to the fleet, and, having cast off the majority[2] of our transports at Shanghai, we take up our fresh and *last* "order of march."

Ahead, in wedge formation, was the scout division consisting of three ships—the *Svietlana*, *Almaz*, and *Ural*; next came the fleet in two columns. The starboard column consisted of the 1st and 2nd armoured squadrons, *i.e.* eight ships—the *Suvoroff*, *Alexander*, *Borodino*, *Orel*,[3] *Sissoy*, *Navarin*, *Nakhimoff*. On the port side were the 3rd armoured and cruiser squadrons, *i.e.* eight ships—the *Nicolay*, *Senyavin*, *Apraxin*, *Ushakoff*, and the cruisers, *Oleg*, *Aurora*, *Donskoy*, and *Monomakh*. On either beam, and parallel with the leading ships, were the *Zemtchug* and *Izumrud*, each accompanied by two torpedo-boats, acting as scouts for the port and starboard columns. In rear of, and between, the wakes of these columns steamed a line of transports which we *were obliged* to take to Vladivostok[4]—the *Anadir*, *Irtish*, *Korea*, *Kamchatka*—and with them the repair and steam-tugs, *Svir* and *Russ*, ready to render assistance in case of need. With the cruiser squadron were five torpedo-boats, whose duty it was to co-operate with the former in protecting the transports during the battle. Astern of all came the hospital ships, *Orel* and *Kostroma*.

This disposition of the fleet would make it possible, if the enemy appeared unexpectedly, for the various squadrons to take order of battle quickly and without any complicated manoeuvres (*i.e.* without attracting attention). The scout division was to turn from whichever side the enemy appeared and to join the cruisers, which were to convoy the transports out of action, and protect them from the enemy's cruisers. The 1st and 2nd armoured squadrons were to increase speed, and, having inclined to port *together*,[5] were to take station in front of the 3rd armoured squadron and proceed on their former course. The result would be that the three squadrons would then be in single column line ahead, and the centre of our fleet would consist of twelve armoured ships. The *Zemtchug* and *Izumrud* were to manoeuvre according to circumstances and, taking advantage of their speed, together with the torpedo-boats assigned to them, were to take station ahead, astern, or abeam of the armoured ships. They were to be on the further side of the fleet from the enemy, out of the range of his shells; their duty being to prevent the enemy's torpedo-boats from getting round the fleet.

Above was the plan of battle, worked out beforehand and known to every officer in the fleet. The various details as to formations dependent on the direction in which the enemy appeared, the instructions for fire control, the manner in which assistance was to be rendered to injured ships, the transfer of the Admiral's flag from one ship to another, the handing over of the command, etc., etc., were laid down in special orders issued by the Commander-in-Chief, but these details would scarcely be of interest to readers unacquainted with naval matters.

The day (25th May) passed quietly. Towards evening it was reported that an accident had happened to the *Senyavin's* engines, and all that night we steamed slowly. In the ward-room of the *Suvoroff* the officers grumbled and swore at the "old tubs,"[6] as they nicknamed Nebogatoff's ships, but, although natural, it was hardly fair, for we ourselves were little better. The prolonged voyage had been a long mournful indictment of our boilers and machinery, while our martyrs of engineers had literally had to "get oil out of flints," and to effect repairs although with no material at hand with which to make them.

That night, the first cold one after six months in the tropics, we slept splendidly, but, of course, by watches, *i.e.* half the night one half of the officers and crew were at the guns, and the other half the remainder.

On 26th May the clouds began to break and the sun shone fitfully, but although a fairly fresh south-westerly breeze had sprung up, a thick mist still lay upon the water.

Being anxious to avail himself of every moment of daylight while passing the Japanese coast, where we would most probably be attacked by torpedoes, the Admiral arranged for the fleet to be in the centre of its passage through the straits of Tsu-shima at noon on the 27th May. According to our calculations this would give us about four hours to spare, which we employed in practising manoeuvres for the last time.

Once again, and for the *last* time, we were forcibly reminded of the old truism that a "fleet" is created by long years of practice at sea in time of peace (cruising, not remaining in port), and, that a collection of ships of various types hastily collected, which have only learned to sail together on the way to the scene of operations, is no fleet, but a chance concourse of vessels.

Taking up order of battle was moderately performed, but it was spoilt by the 3rd squadron, and who can blame its admiral or captains? When near Madagascar, and during our wanderings off the coast of Annam, our ships to a certain extent had been able to learn their work, and to get to know one another. They had, in fact, been able to "rehearse." But as the 3rd squadron, which joined the fleet barely a fortnight ago,[7] had only arrived in time to finish the voyage with us and take part in the battle, there was no time for it to receive instruction.

Admiral Togo, on the other hand, had commanded his squadron continuously for eight years without hauling down his flag. Five of the vice-admirals and seven of the rear-admirals taking part in the Tsu-shima battle, in command of squadrons, ships, or as junior flag officers, were his old comrades and pupils, having been educated under his command. As for us, we could only regret our unpreparedness, and in the coming fight there was nothing for us to do but to make the most of what we had.

Rozhdestvensky thought (and facts later fully justified the opinion) that in the decisive battle Togo would be at the head of his twelve best armoured ships. Against them our Admiral was also to lead twelve similar ships (which he handled magnificently), and in the duel between them it was thought the centre of gravity of the fight would certainly lie. The difference between our main force and that of the Japanese was very material. The oldest of Togo's twelve ships—the *Fuji*, was two years younger than the *Sissoy*, which, among our twelve best, came sixth in seniority! Their speed was one-and-a-half times as great as ours, but their chief superiority lay in their new shells, of which we had no inkling.

What with manoeuvres, etc., the 26th May passed almost imperceptibly.

I do not know the feeling on board the other ships, but in the *Suvoroff* we were cheerful and eager for the fray. Anxious, of course, we were, but not so over-anxious as to worry. The officers went their rounds, and looked after their men more than usual; explained details, talked, and found fault with those immediately under them more than was their wont. Some, the thought suddenly occurring to them, put their keepsakes and the letters which they had just written into the treasure chest for safety.

"He evidently means to leave us!" said Lieutenant Vladimirsky, the senior gunnery officer, pointing to a sailor who was busy rummaging in a bag.

"What! made your preparations for going already?"

"I?" said he in amazement; and with a grin—"Yes—I am quite ready!"

"Look here!" said Lieutenant Bogdanoff, the senior torpedo officer, who was a veteran of the former war and had been wounded at the capture of the Taku forts—"To-morrow—or rather to-night—you'll please go to the office and get your accounts made up!"

This humour had no effect.

"And haven't *you* a presentiment? *You've* been under fire before," asked a young sub-lieutenant, coming up, with his hand in his pocket, in which was evidently a letter destined for the treasure chest.

Bogdanoff got annoyed. "What do you mean by a presentiment? I'm not your fortune-teller! I tell you what! If Japanese guns begin talking to us to-morrow you will feel something soon enough,—but you won't feel anything before then!"[8]

Some more officers approached. Times without number we had hotly discussed the question,—would we meet the whole of the Japanese fleet at Tsu-shima, or only part of it?

Optimists asserted that Togo would be misled, and would patrol to the North to look out for us, as the *Terek* and *Kuban* had on the 22nd gone round the eastern shores of Japan endeavouring to attract as much attention there as possible.[9]

Pessimists declared that Togo was as well able as we were to understand the conditions, and would know that a single coaling was not sufficient to enable us to steam all round Japan; we should have to coal again. And where? We were no longer in the tropics; the weather here was anything but reliable, which meant we could not count upon coaling at sea. Take shelter in some bay?—but there were telegraph stations, and, of course, intelligence posts, everywhere. Togo would learn of it in good time, so what would he gain by hastening northward? Even if we succeeded in coaling at sea and slipped unnoticed into one of the Straits, we couldn't conceal our movements there, thanks to their narrowness. And then—submarine and floating mines, sown along our course, and attacks by torpedo-boats, which would be easy even in broad daylight!

It was impossible to pass unnoticed through these Straits even in a fog or in bad weather; how then could a fleet accompanied by transports hope to escape observation? Even if the Almighty did bring us through all this, what was beyond?—the meeting with the Japanese fleet which from Tsu-shima could always come out across our course while our fleet would have already been harassed in the Straits by torpedo-boats as well as every conceivable type of mine.

"Gentlemen—Gentlemen! let me speak!" exclaimed the first lieutenant and senior navigating officer, Zotoff, who was always fond of discussions and liked making his voice heard. "It is quite clear that the best course for us is up the eastern side of the gulf of Korea. My chief reason for saying so is because here it is wide and deep, while there is room for us to manoeuvre, and it can be navigated without danger in any weather. In fact, the worse the weather the better for us. All this has been talked over till nothing more remains to be said, and considered till nothing is left to consider; even disciples of Voltaire themselves would admit this. Presumably Togo is no greater fool than we, and knows this. I assume that he also knows how to use a pair of compasses and is acquainted with the four rules of arithmetic! This being so he can easily calculate that, if we steam round Japan, deciding in the face of our knowledge to brave the mines before meeting him, it would still be possible for him to intercept us on the road to Vladivostok, if, at the same time as we come out of the ocean into the Straits, he starts from ... Attention, gentlemen! ... from the northernmost point of Tsu-shima. There is no doubt that arrangements have been made to organise a defence of the Straits by mines. The naval ports of Aomori and Mororan are on either side. If any one doesn't know it he ought to be ashamed of himself. Togo may tell off some of his smaller mining vessels to go there, but he, with his main force (I would even go so far as to say with the whole of his fleet)—where will he be? No, I will put another question: Where ought he to be? Why! nowhere else but off the northern point of Tsu-shima. He can gain nothing by loitering about at sea, so he will be lying in some bay."

"In Mazampo, for instance?" asked Sub-Lieutenant Ball, the junior navigating officer.

"Mazampo—if you like—but let me finish. It is childish to hope that the Japanese main fleet will be out of the way. I think we have reached the culminating point of our adventures. To-morrow the decision must be made: either vertically"—and, putting his hand above his head, he energetically waved it downwards in front of him—"or"—quietly moving his arm out to the right, and dropping it slowly downwards in a circular direction—"a longer route, but to the west all the same."

"How? Why? Why to the west?" broke in the bystanders.

"Because though the end may not come at once," shouted Zotoff, "the result will be the same! It's absurd to think of steaming victoriously into Vladivostok, or of getting command of the sea! The only possible chance is a dash through! and having dashed through, after two, three, or at the most four sallies, we shall have burnt all our supplies of coal, and have shed our blossoms before we have bloomed! We shall have to prepare for a siege, take our guns on shore, teach the crew to use bayonets——"

"A bas! A bas! Conspuez le prophête!" interrupted some. "Hear! Hear! strongly[10] said!" shouted others. "What about Austria's Parliament!"

"Let him finish," growled Bogdanoff in his bass voice.

"Having postponed a discussion of questions of the distant future—a discussion which makes those who take part in it so excited," continued Zotoff, availing himself of a quiet moment, "I will venture to say a few words concerning what is immediately at hand. I foresee three possibilities. Firstly:—If we have already been discovered, or are discovered in the course of the day, we shall certainly be subjected at night to a series of torpedo attacks, and in the morning shall have to fight the Japanese fleet, which will be unpleasant. Secondly:—If we are not discovered till to-morrow we shall be able to commence the fight at full strength, without casualties, which will be better. Lastly, and thirdly:—If the mist thickens and dirty weather comes on, thanks to the width of the Straits, we may either slip through, or be discovered too late, when there will be only the open sea between us and Vladivostok.—This would be excellent. On these three chances those who wish may start the totalisator! For myself, preparing for the worst, and foreseeing a broken night, I suggest that we all take advantage of every spare hour to sleep."

His words had the desired effect.

CHAPTER II

Fate had apparently been kind to us, as up to the present we had not been discovered. The sending of telegrams in the fleet was forbidden, so we were able to intercept Japanese messages, and our torpedo officers made every effort to fix the direction from which they emanated. On the morning of 26th May and later on the same day, a conversation between two installations had begun, or perhaps more correctly speaking it was the reports of one ahead of and nearer to us to which the other, more distant and on the port side, was replying. The messages were not in cypher, and although our telegraphists were unaccustomed to the strange alphabet, and notwithstanding the gaps in the sentences by the time we received them, it was still possible to pick out separate words, and even sentences. "Last night" ... "nothing" ... "eleven lights ... but not in line" ... "bright light ... the same star ..." etc.

In all probability this was a powerful coast station on the Goto Islands, reporting to some one a long way off what had been seen in the Straits.

Towards evening we took in a conversation between other installations, which at night had increased to seven. The messages were in cypher, but by their brevity and uniformity and by the fact that they commenced and ceased at fixed times, we were able to calculate with tolerable accuracy that these were not reports, but merely messages exchanged between the scouts. It was clear that we had not been discovered.

At sunset the fleet closed up, and in expectation of torpedo attacks half the officers and crew were detailed for duty at the guns, the remainder sleeping by their posts, without undressing, ready to jump up on the first sound of the alarm.

The night came on dark. The mist seemed to grow denser, and through it but few stars could be seen. On the dark deck there prevailed a strained stillness, broken at times only by the sighs of the sleepers, the steps of an officer, or by an order given in an undertone. Near the guns the motionless figures of their crews seemed like dead, but all were wide awake, gazing keenly into the darkness. Was not that the dark shadow of a torpedo-boat? They listened attentively. Surely the throb of her engines and the noise of steam must betray an invisible foe?

Stepping carefully, so as not to disturb the sleepers, I went round the bridges and decks, and then proceeded to the engine-room. For a moment the bright light blinded me. Here, life and movement was visible on all sides. Men were nimbly running up and down the ladders; there was a tinkling of bells and buzzing of voices. Orders were being transmitted loudly, but, on looking more intently, the tension and anxiety—that same peculiar frame of mind so noticeable on deck—could also be observed. And then it suddenly occurred to me that all this—the tall, somewhat bent figure of the Admiral on the side of the bridge, the wrinkled face of the man at the wheel stooping over the compass, the guns' crews chilled to the bone at their posts, these men talking loudly and running about, the giant connecting-rods whose steel glittered dimly in the dark, and the mighty hissing of steam in the cylinders—was one and the same thing.

I suddenly remembered the old sea legend of the ship's spirit dwelling in every rivet, nail, and screw, which at the fated moment takes possession of the whole ship with her crew, and turns both crew and surroundings into one indivisible supernatural being. Of a sudden it seemed that this spirit was looking right into my heart, which beat with unusual rapidity, and for a moment it seemed as if I had become this being to whom the name *Suvoroff*—so sacred to all of us—was no more than a mere rivet!

It was a flash of madness, which quickly passed, leaving behind it only a sensation akin to daring and grim determination.

Alongside of me, the chief engineer, Captain Bernander, my old shipmate and friend, was angrily explaining something to his assistant. I did not hear what he said, nor could I understand why he was so excited when everything had been finally settled. Whether for better or for worse it was impossible to alter things now.

"All in good time, my dear fellow," said I, taking his arm. "Let us go and drink some tea—my throat is parched."

Turning his kind grey eyes on me in astonishment, and without replying, he allowed me to lead him away.

We went up to the ward-room, which at this hour was usually crowded and noisy. It was empty. Two or three officers, after being relieved, as well as some from the nearest light gun batteries, were sound asleep on the sofas, awaiting the alarm, or for their turn to go on watch. The messman, however, who was always ready for any emergency, brought us tea. Again on all sides this dreadful, painful stillness.

"The chief thing is, not to be in too great a hurry.—One straight shot is better than two bad ones.—Remember that we have not a single spare shell, and, till we reach Vladivostok, none are to be got," came in a somewhat inaudible voice from behind the closed door of the stern cabin. Evidently a sub-lieutenant, Fomin by name, was holding forth.

"Preaching!" angrily said Bernander, helping himself to some hot tea.

I saw that he was very annoyed about something and wished to unburden himself.

"Well! tell me all about it! What is the matter?"

"It is all this cursed German coal," he said, and lowering his voice and looking rounds—"You know, of course, that we had a fire in the bunkers?"

"Yes! I know; but surely, thank goodness, they put it out? Do you mean there's another?"

"No! Not quite! Listen! There's a vast difference between rapid-burning and slow-burning coal. Much more is consumed. Compared to good coal, 20 to 30 per cent.——"

"Shut up!" I interrupted. "Why, what's up with you? Are you afraid you'll run out? Up till now, surely, you have been burning our surplus! You ought to have in hand the full normal quantity."

"Full or not, we shall have less than 1000 tons by morning."

"But it's 600 miles to Vladivostok! Where do you want to go?"

"Have you forgotten the *Cesarevitch*? On 10th August, when her funnels were shot away, she burnt 480 tons in the twenty-four hours! Well—we are burning more!"

"Pooh! your nerves are unstrung," I exclaimed. "All your bunkers haven't caught fire!"

"You don't understand!" angrily exclaimed Bernander, and, quickly finishing his tea, he seized his cap and went out.

I remained in the ward-room, settled myself down in an easy-chair, and, making myself comfortable, dozed. I heard indistinctly the watch being relieved at midnight. Some of the officers coming off duty came in to get some tea, and in low voices abused the infernal rawness of the night air. Others stretched themselves on sofas, sighing with relief at being so comfortable, and said: "We'll sleep till four! it's a holiday at home!"

I also went to sleep.

About 3 A.M. I awoke, and again went round the ship and up on deck. The scene was just the same as in the evening, but it was lighter. In the last quarter the moon had risen well up, and against the mist, dimly whitened by its silver rays, the ship's funnels, masts, and rigging were sharply outlined. The breeze, freshening, blew cold, making me pull the cape of my coat more over my head.

Going on to the fore-bridge, I found the Admiral sleeping in a chair. The Commander, wearing soft slippers, was pacing rapidly but quietly up and down the bridge.

"What are you doing wandering about?" he asked me.

"O, just having a look round. Gone to sleep?" and I nodded towards the Admiral.

"Only just. I persuaded him to. Why shouldn't he? We can take it that the night has passed all right. Up to the present we haven't been discovered. They are still calling each other up, and now, even though they do find us, it's late. It will be daybreak in a couple of hours. Even if their torpedo-boats are near us, they won't be able to collect. Besides, how can they find us in weather like this? Look! you can't even see the rear of the fleet! It's 200,000 to 1 against any one running into us accidentally! But I don't like the breeze. It's freshening. Let's hope it won't break up the mist. If it does to-morrow will mean the end of the *Suvoroff*. But it's suddenly coming on thicker," he said eagerly. "Why, we have been going for twenty-four hours without being seen. If it is the same to-morrow, we'll give them the slip! They are on the move, and keep calling each other up, and they haven't yet come on us! They'll have to wait for our second coming, out of Vladivostok! That'll be a different tale. My! what a stew they must be in! What fun!" and putting his handkerchief in his mouth so as not to disturb the Admiral, he laughed so heartily, and seemed so free from care, that I envied him.

It should be stated that V. V. Ignatzius, in the first place, was one of those who was firmly convinced that the success of our voyage—this desperate adventure—depended solely on the extent of co-operation of Saint Nicolas "The Casual" and other heavenly powers, and, in the second place, bearing in mind the Japanese custom of concentrating their fire on the flag-ship, he believed that both he and his ship were doomed to destruction in the first decisive engagement. But, in spite of this, he never for a moment lost his invariably buoyant and cheery manner. He joked, chaffed, and eagerly threw himself into all the little details of daily life on board, while now (I really believe) he was, inwardly, much amused, picturing to himself the anger and disappointment of the Japanese in the event of our actually slipping past them.

But the Japanese "got the 200,000th chance," and more.

At dawn on 27th May, about 5 A.M., the auxiliary cruiser *Sinano Maru* almost ran into our hospital ships, and it was due to this that the whole fleet was discovered. We were unable to see what had happened, but by the changed character of the messages it became at once apparent that our presence was known. The scouts no longer merely called each other up, and we now took in reports, which were being transmitted further and further to the north.[11]

Messages came in from both sides, so the Admiral recalled the *Almaz, Svietlana* and *Ural*, in order to protect our helpless rear (transports) from sudden attack.

About 6 A.M. the *Ural* came up at full speed, reporting by semaphore that astern of the fleet four ships, which it was impossible to recognise in the mist, were crossing from starboard to port.

At 6.45 A.M. a vessel appeared on the starboard beam, which, as her course brought her nearer to us, was soon recognised as the *Idzumi*. About 8 A.M., despite the mist, we were able to take her distance as 10,000 yards. The alarm sounding, the after turret threateningly raised her 12-inch guns, but the *Idzumi*, guessing her danger, commenced rapidly to beat a retreat.

We might, of course, have detached a good cruiser to drive her off, but alas! there were in the fleet only two ships answering to this description—the *Oleg* and the *Aurora*, also possibly the scout *Svietlana*; of the remainder, the *Donskoy* and *Monomakh* were respectable veterans, slow, though passably armed. The *Ural* and *Almaz* were swift, but had only toy guns. Besides, each moment we were expecting to meet our formidable opponent, when every gun and shell would be of value. If the issue of the battle were to be decided by a duel between our three armoured squadrons and the twelve best Japanese ships, the whole of the rest of the enemy's fleet would fall to the lot of our cruiser squadron. A struggle for which we must indeed reserve our strength! Rozhdestvensky decided accordingly to ignore the *Idzumi's* daring sally, and sent no one in pursuit of her.

Shortly after 8 A.M., on the port bow, the *Chin-Yen*, *Matsushima*, *Itsukushima*, and *Hashidate* appeared out of the mist, steaming on an almost parallel course. Ahead of them was a small, light cruiser, apparently the *Akitsushu*, which hurriedly drew off to the north as soon as we were able to see her well (and equally she us), and the whole squadron began slowly to increase their distance and gradually to disappear from sight.

At about 10 A.M. the light cruisers *Chitose*, *Kasagi*, *Niitaka*, and *Otawa*, also appeared on the port beam, and it became evident to all of us that the decisive moment could not now be long postponed.

At a signal from the flag-ship, the 1st and 2nd armoured squadrons steamed ahead, and, turning "together," 2 points[12] to port, began to take position ahead of the 3rd squadron. The transports were ordered to keep more to starboard and astern of the fleet, while the cruisers were to cover them on the port side. To starboard of the transports was the *Monomakh*, detailed to protect them from the *Idzumi* and suchlike vessels.

At 11.20 A.M., when the distance of the Japanese light cruisers was 10,000 yards, the *Orel* fired an accidental shot (which she immediately reported by semaphore). Unable with smokeless powder to tell by which of the leading ships it had been fired, the fleet took it as a signal from the *Suvoroff*, and opened fire. Of the whole fleet the fire of the 3rd squadron was the heaviest.

The Japanese cruisers turned to port and, firing also, rapidly drew off. The flag-ship then signalled, "*Ammunition not to be wasted*," and when the firing ceased, "Ships' companies to have dinner at once."

At midday, finding ourselves on a line with the southernmost point of Tsu-shima, we shaped course N.23°E. for Vladivostok.

The officers also had breakfast now, in turn, and as quickly as possible. To-day there was to have been as usual a big breakfast in the ward-room, with the Admiral and his Captain and staff as guests: but on this occasion it naturally could not take place as the Admiral and Captain were unable to leave the bridge, and the staff only dashed down to the Admiral's table to eat a few mouthfuls.

Having gone down to my cabin to fill my cigarette-case before the fight, I happened to look in at the ward-room at the psychological minute. Although the dishes were being handed anyhow and whatever came nearest was taken, champagne sparkled in the glasses, and every one was standing up, silently listening to the toast proposed by the senior officer, A. P. Makedonsky.

"On this, the great anniversary of the sacred Coronation of their Highnesses, may God help us to serve with honour our beloved Country! To the health of the Emperor! the Empress!—To Russia!"

The ward-room resounded with cheers, and their last echoes had scarcely died away ere the alarm sounded on deck. Every one rushed to their stations, to find that some Japanese light cruisers had again appeared on our port bow, but this time they were accompanied by torpedo-boats, which evidently intended to cross our bows. Suspecting that their plan was to lay floating mines (as they had done on 10th August), the Admiral ordered the 1st squadron to turn to starboard, so as to drive off the enemy by threatening him with the fire of our five best battleships.

With this intention the ships of the 1st squadron turned "in succession" 8 points (90°) to starboard, and should afterwards have turned "together" 8 points to port. The first half of the manoeuvre was most successfully performed, but the signal for the second was evidently misunderstood, as the *Alexander* followed the *Suvoroff,* while the *Borodino* and *Orel,* which had already commenced to turn correctly "together," imagining then that they were mistaken, turned back and followed the *Alexander.* Consequently the 1st squadron found itself in single column line ahead, parallel to the 2nd and 3rd squadrons, but somewhat ahead of them.

This unsuccessful manoeuvre, however, had a most important result. The enemy's cruisers and torpedo-boats, afraid of being caught between the fire of both columns, abandoned their intention of crossing our course, and hurriedly drew off to port. These cruisers probably also reported to Togo that we were steaming in two columns, and he (being then out of sight and far ahead of us on the starboard bow) decided to cross over to our port side, so as to throw himself with all his strength upon our port and weakest column.

As soon as the Japanese drew off, the 1st squadron at once increased speed, inclining to port so as again to take station ahead of the 2nd squadron.

At 1.20 P.M., when the 1st had got ahead of the 2nd and 3rd squadrons and was steering on its former course, the flag-ship signalled, "The 2nd squadron, maintaining its formation, will take station astern of the 1st."

And now, far ahead of us in the distance, could be dimly seen approaching through the mist the Japanese main force. Their ships were crossing our bows from starboard to port, following on an almost south-west course. The *Mikasa*, as soon as she crossed our bows, at once altered course to the southward, followed by the *Shikishima*, *Fuji*, Asahi, *Kasuga*, and *Nisshin*.

Meanwhile, though the flag-ship was already being worked from the conning tower, Rozhdestvensky was still standing with his staff on the upper fore-bridge.

I frankly confess that I did not agree with his opinion as to Togo leading all his twelve armoured ships in column; on 10th August he ordered six of them to work independently, instead of joining his squadron. I was inclined to think that Kamimura would operate independently and, when my six old Port Arthur acquaintances hove in sight, I said triumphantly:

"There they are, sir—*all six*—just as on 10th August."

But Rozhdestvensky, without turning, shook his head.

"No, there are more—they are all there," and he went down into the conning tower.

"To your stations, gentlemen," said the Flag Captain quickly, as he followed the Admiral.

And there, sure enough, following after the first six ships, and slowly appearing out of the mist, came the *Idzumo*, *Yakumo*, *Asama*, *Adzuma*, *Tokiwa*, and *Iwate*.

CHAPTER III

"Now the fun will begin," thought I to myself, going up to the after-bridge, which seemed to be the most convenient place for carrying out my duty of seeing and noting down everything, as from there I could see both the enemy and our own fleet. Lieutenant Reydkin, commanding the after starboard 6-inch turret, was also there, having dashed up to see what was going on, as the fight was apparently to commence to port, and his turret would not be in action.

We stood side by side, exchanging now and again abrupt remarks, not understanding why the Japanese intended crossing to our port side, when our weak spot—the transports and cruisers covering them—was astern, and to starboard of us. Perhaps, having commenced the fight while steering on the opposite course, and having taken advantage of their superior speed, they calculated on rounding us from the stern, in order to fall at the same time on our transports and weak rear! If so, a raking fire would present no difficulties.

"Hullo! Look! What *are* they up to?" said Reydkin, and his voice betrayed both delight and amazement.

I looked and looked, and, not believing my eyes, could not put down my glasses. The Japanese ships had suddenly commenced to turn "in succession" to port, reversing their course!

If the reader recollects what has been said previously on the subject of turns, he will easily understand that this manoeuvre made it necessary for all the enemy's ships to pass in succession over the point on which the leading ship had turned; this point was, so to speak, stationary on the water, making it easy for us to range and aim. Besides—even with a speed of 15 knots, the manoeuvre must take about fifteen minutes to complete, and all this time the vessels, which had already turned, would mask the fire of those which were still coming up.

"*How* rash!" said Reydkin, who could not keep quiet. "Why, in a minute we'll be able to roll up the leading ships!"

"Please God, we may!" thought I.

It was plain to me that Togo, seeing something which he had not expected, had suddenly changed his mind. The manoeuvre was undoubtedly risky, but, on the other hand, if he found it necessary to steer on the opposite course, there was no other way of doing it. He might have ordered the fleet to turn "together," but this would have made the cruiser *Iwate* the leading ship in action, which he evidently did not wish. Togo accordingly decided to turn "in succession," in order that he should lead the fleet in person, and not leave success at the commencement of the action to depend upon the presence of mind and enterprise of the junior flag-officer. (The *Iwate* flew Rear-Admiral Simamura's flag.)

My heart beat furiously, as it had never done before during the six months at Port Arthur. If we succeeded! God grant it! Even though we didn't sink one of them, if we could only put one out of action! The first success—was it possible?

Meanwhile Rozhdestvensky hastened to avail himself of this favourable opportunity.

At *1.49 p.m.*, when the manoeuvre had been performed by the *Mikasa* and *Shikishima* (two only out of the twelve), the *Suvoroff* fired the first shot at a range of 6,400 yards, and the guns of the whole fleet thundered forth. I watched closely through my glasses. The shots which went over and those which fell short were all close, but the most interesting, *i.e.* the hits, as in the fight of 10th August, could not be seen. Our shells on bursting emitted scarcely any smoke, and the fuses were adjusted to burst inside after penetrating the target. A hit could only be detected when something fell—and nothing fell! In a couple of minutes, when the *Fuji* and *Asahi* had turned also and were following the first ships, the enemy began to reply.

The first shells flew over us. At this range some of the long ones turned a complete somersault, and could clearly be seen with the naked eye curving like so many sticks thrown in the air. They flew over us, making a sort of wail, different to the ordinary roar.

"Are those the portmanteaus?"[13] I asked Reydkin, smiling.

"Yes. Those are they."

But what struck me most was that these "portmanteaus," curving awkwardly head over heels through the air and falling anyhow on the water, exploded the moment they touched its surface. This had never happened before.

After them came others short of us—nearer and nearer. Splinters whistled through the air, jingled against the side and superstructure. Then, quite close and abreast the foremost funnel, rose a gigantic pillar of smoke, water and flame. I saw stretchers being carried along the fore-bridge, and I leaned over the rail.

"Prince Tsereteli!"[14] shouted Reydkin from below, in reply to my silent question, as he went towards his turret.

The next shell struck the side by the centre 6-inch turret, and there was a tremendous noise behind and below me on the port quarter. Smoke and tongues of fire leapt out of the officers' gangway; a shell having fallen into the captain's cabin, and having penetrated the deck, had burst in the officers' quarters, setting them on fire.

And here I was able to observe, and not for the first time, the stupor which seems to come over men, who have never been in action before, when the first shells begin to fall. A stupor which turns easily and instantaneously, at the most insignificant external shock, into either uncontrollable panic which cannot be allayed, or into unusually high spirits, depending on the man's character.

The men at the fire mains and hoses stood as if mesmerised, gazing at the smoke and flames, not understanding, apparently, what was happening. I went down to them from the bridge, and with the most commonplace words, such as "Wake up! Turn the water on!"—got them to pull themselves together and bravely to fight the fire.

I was taking out my watch and pocket-book to make a note of the first fire, when something suddenly struck me in the waist, and something large and soft, though heavy, hit me in the back, lifting me up and hurling me on to the deck. When I again got up, my note-book and watch were in my hands as before. My watch was going; but the second hand was slightly bent, and the glass had disappeared. Stupefied by the blow, and not myself, I began carefully to hunt for it on the deck, and found it unbroken. Picking it up, I fitted it in to my watch—and, only then realising that I had been occupied with something of no importance, I looked round.

I had probably been unconscious for some time, as the fire had been extinguished, and, save for two or three dead bodies on which water was pouring from the torn hoses, no one was to be seen. Whatever had struck me had come from the direction of the deck house aft, which was hidden from me by a mantlet of hammocks. I looked in the direction where the flag-officers, with a party of poop signalmen, should have been. The shell had passed through the deck house, bursting inside. Of the ten or twelve signalmen, some seemed to be standing by the starboard 6-inch turret, others seemed to be lying in a huddled group. Inside was a pile of something, and on the top lay an officer's telescope.

"Is this all that is left?" I wondered, but I was wrong, as by some miracle Novosiltseff and Kozakevitch were only wounded and, helped by Maximoff, had gone to the dressing station, while I was lying on the deck occupied with mending my watch.

"Hullo! a scene that you are accustomed to? Like the 10th August?" said the irrepressible Reydkin, peeping out of his turret.

"Just the same!" I replied in a confident tone. But it was hardly so: indeed, it would have been more correct to say—"Not in the least like."

On 10th August, in a fight lasting some hours, the *Cesarevitch* was struck by only nineteen large shells, and I, in all seriousness, had intended in the present engagement to note the times and the places where we were hit, as well as the damage done. But how could I make detailed notes when it seemed impossible even to count the number of projectiles striking us? I had not only never witnessed such a fire before, but I had never imagined anything like it. Shells seemed to be pouring upon us incessantly, one after another.[15]

After six months with the Port Arthur squadron I had grown indifferent to most things. Shimose and melinite were to a certain extent old acquaintances, but this was something new. It seemed as if these were mines, not shells, which were striking the ship's side and falling on the deck. They burst as soon as they touched anything—the moment they encountered the least impediment in their flight. Handrails, funnel guys, topping lifts of the boats' derricks, were quite sufficient to cause a thoroughly efficient burst. The steel plates and superstructure on the upper deck were torn to pieces, and the splinters caused many casualties. Iron ladders were crumpled up into rings, and guns were literally hurled from their mountings.

Such havoc would never be caused by the simple impact of a shell, still less by that of its splinters. It could only be caused by the force of the explosion. The Japanese had apparently succeeded in realising what the Americans had endeavoured to attain in inventing their "Vesuvium."

In addition to this, there was the unusual high temperature and liquid flame of the explosion, which seemed to spread over everything. I actually watched a steel plate catch fire from a burst. Of course, the steel did not burn, but the paint on it did. Such almost non-combustible materials as hammocks, and rows of boxes, drenched with water, flared up in a moment. At times it was impossible to see anything with glasses, owing to everything being so distorted with the quivering, heated air. No! It was different to the 10th August![16]

I hurriedly went to the Admiral in the conning tower. Why? At the time I did not attempt to think, but now feel sure that I merely wished to see him, and by seeing him to confirm my impressions. Was it all imagination? Was it all a nightmare? Had I become jumpy?

Running along the fore-bridge I almost fell, slipping in a pool of blood (the chief signalman—Kandaooroff—had just been killed there). I went into the conning tower, and found the Admiral and Captain both bending down, looking out through the chink between the armour and the roof.

"Sir," said the Captain, energetically gesticulating as was his wont, "we must shorten the distance. They're all being killed—they are on fire!"

"Wait a bit. Aren't we all being killed also?" replied the Admiral.

Close to the wheel, and on either side of it, lay two bodies in officers' tunics—face downwards.

"The officer at the wheel, and Berseneff!"[17] was shouted in my ear by a sub-lieutenant—Shishkin—whose arm I had touched, pointing to the bodies. "Berseneff first—in the head—quite dead."

The range-finder was worked. Vladimirsky shouted his orders in a clear voice, and the electricians quickly turned the handles of the indicator, transmitting the range to the turrets and light gun batteries.

"We're all right," thought I to myself, going out of the conning tower, but the next moment the thought flashed across me: "They can't see what is going on on board." Leaving the tower, I looked out intently on all sides from the fore-bridge. Were not my recent thoughts, which I had not dared to put into words, realised?

No!

The enemy had finished turning. His twelve ships were in perfect order at close intervals, steaming parallel to us, but gradually forging ahead. No disorder was noticeable. It seemed to me that with my Zeiss glasses (the distance was a little more than 4,000 yards), I could even distinguish the mantlets of hammocks on the bridges, and groups of men. But with us? I looked round. What havoc!—Burning bridges, smouldering *débris* on the decks,—piles of dead bodies. Signalling and judging distance stations, gun-directing positions, all were destroyed. And astern of us the *Alexander* and *Borodino* were also enveloped in smoke. No! it was very different to the 10th August.

The enemy, steaming ahead, commenced quickly to incline to starboard, endeavouring to cross our T. We also bore to starboard, and again we had him almost on our beam.

It was now 2.5 p.m.

A man came up to report what had taken place in the after 12-inch turret. I went to look. Part of the shield over the port gun had been torn off and bent upwards, but the turret was still turning and keeping up a hot fire.

The officer commanding the fire parties had had both his legs blown off and was carried below. Men fell faster and faster. Reinforcements were required everywhere to replace casualties, even at the turrets into which splinters could only penetrate through the narrow gun ports. The dead were, of course, left to lie where they had fallen, but yet there were not enough men to look after the wounded.

There are no spare men on board a warship, and a reserve does not exist. Each man is detailed for some particular duty, and told off to his post in action. The only source which we could tap was the crews of the 47 millimetre, and machine, guns, who from the commencement of the fight had been ordered to remain below the armoured deck so as not to be unnecessarily exposed. Having nothing to do now, as all their guns, which were in exposed positions on the bridges, had been utterly destroyed, we made use of them, but they were a mere drop in the ocean. As for the fires, even if we had had the men, we were without the means with which to fight them. Over and over again the hoses in use were changed for new ones, but these also were soon torn to ribbons, and the supply became exhausted. Without hoses how could we pump water on to the bridges and spar-deck where the flames raged? On the spar-deck, in particular, where eleven wooden boats were piled up, the fire was taking a firm hold. Up till now, this "store of wood" had only caught fire in places, as the water which had been poured into the boats prior to the commencement of the action was still in them, though it was fast trickling out of the numerous cracks momentarily being made by the splinters.

We, of course, did everything possible: tried to plug the holes, and brought up water in buckets.[18] I am not certain if the scuppers had been closed on purpose, or had merely become blocked, but practically none of the water we used for the fire ran overboard, and it lay, instead, on the upper deck. This was fortunate, as, in the first place, the deck itself did not catch fire, and, in the second, we threw into it the smouldering *débris* falling from above—merely separating the burning pieces and turning them over.

Seeing Flag Sub-Lieutenant Demchinsky standing by the ladder of the fore-bridge, with a party of forecastle signalmen near the starboard forward 6-inch turret, I went up to him. Golovnin, another sub-lieutenant, who was in charge of the turret, gave us some cold tea to drink, which he had stored in bottles. It seems a trifle, but it cheered us up.

Demchinsky told me that the first shell striking the ship had fallen right into the temporary dressing station, rigged up by the doctor in what seemed the most sheltered spot on the upper battery (between the centre 6-inch turrets by the ship's ikon). He said that it had caused a number of casualties; that the doctor somehow escaped, but the ship's chaplain had been dangerously wounded. I went there to have a look at the place.

The ship's ikon or, more properly speaking, ikons as there were several of them, all farewell gifts to the ship, were untouched. The glass of the big ikon case had not even been broken, and in front of it, on hanging candlesticks, candles were peacefully burning. There wasn't a soul to be seen. Between the wrecked tables, stools, broken bottles, and different hospital appliances were some dead bodies, and a mass of something, which, with difficulty, I guessed to be the remains of what had once been men.

I had not had time properly to take in this scene of destruction when Demchinsky came down the ladder, supporting Flag Lieutenant Sverbeyeff, who could scarcely stand.

He was gasping for breath, and asked for water. Ladling some out of a bucket into a mess kettle, I gave him some, and, as he was unable to use his arms, we had to help him. He drank greedily, jerking out a few words—"It's a trifle—tell the Flag Captain—I'll come immediately—I am suffocated with these cursed gases—I'll get my breath in a minute." He inhaled the air with a great effort through his blue lips, and something seemed to rattle in his throat and chest, though not, of course, the poisonous gases. On the right side of his back his coat was torn in a great rent, and his wound was bleeding badly. Demchinsky told off a couple of men to take him down to the hospital, and we again went on deck.

I crossed over to the port side, between the forward 12-inch and 6-inch turrets, to have a look at the enemy's fleet. It was all there, just the same—no fires—no heeling over—no fallen bridges, as if it had been at drill instead of fighting, and as if our guns, which had been thundering incessantly for the last half-hour, had been firing—not shells, but the devil alone knows what![19]

Feeling almost in despair, I put down my glasses and went aft.

"The last of the halyards are burned," said Demchinsky to me. "I think I shall take my men somewhere under cover." Of course, I fully agreed. What was the use of the signalmen remaining under fire when nothing was left for them to signal with!

It was now 2.20 p.m.

Making my way aft through the *débris*, I met Reydkin hurrying to the forecastle. "We can't fire from the port quarter," he said excitedly; "everything is on fire there, and the men are suffocated with heat and smoke."

"Well! come on, let's get some one to put the fire out."

"I'll do that, but you report to the Admiral. Perhaps he will give us some orders."

"What orders can he give?"

"He may alter the course. I don't know!"

"What! leave the line? Is it likely?"

"Well! anyway, you tell him."

In order to quiet him, I promised to report at once, and we separated, going our ways. As I anticipated, the Admiral only shrugged his shoulders on hearing my report and said, "They *must* put the fire out. No help can be sent from here."

Instead of two dead bodies, five or six were now lying in the conning tower. The man at the wheel having been incapacitated, Vladimirsky had taken his place. His face was covered with blood, but his moustache was smartly twisted upwards, and he wore the same self-confident look as he had in the ward-room when discussing "the future of gunnery."

Leaving the tower, I intended going to Reydkin to tell him the Admiral's reply and to assist in extinguishing the fire, but instead I remained on the bridge looking at the Japanese fleet.

CHAPTER IV

After steering on their new course for a quarter of an hour, the enemy had again forged a considerable distance ahead, and now the *Mikasa*, at the head of the column, gradually inclined to starboard to cross our T. I waited for us to incline to starboard also, but the Admiral held on to the old course for some time longer. I guessed that by doing this he hoped to lessen the distance as much as possible, which would naturally have assisted us, since, with our wrecked range-finders and gun-directing positions, our guns were only serviceable at close quarters. However, to allow the enemy to cross our T and to subject ourselves to a raking fire was not to be thought of. Counting the moments anxiously I watched and waited. The *Mikasa* came closer and closer to our course. Our 6-inch starboard turret was already preparing to fire, when—we sharply inclined to starboard. Breathing freely again, I looked around.

Demchinsky had not yet gone below with his men but was hard at work, apparently moving the cartridge boxes of the 47-millimetre guns off the deck into the turret, so that there should be less risk of their exploding in the fire and causing greater damage. I went to ask him what he was doing, but before I was able to say anything the Captain appeared at the top of the ladder just behind me. His head was covered with blood and, staggering convulsively, he clutched at the hand-rail. At that moment a shell burst quite close to us and, losing his balance from the sudden explosion, he fell, head foremost, down the ladder. Luckily we saw it and were able to catch him.

"It's nothing—only a trifle," he said in his ordinary quick way of speaking. He tried to force a smile and, jumping up, endeavoured to go on. But as to go on to the hospital meant another three ladders, we put him, in spite of his protests, on a stretcher.

A man reported that the after turret had been blown up[20] and almost simultaneously there resounded above us a rumbling noise accompanied by the sharp clank of falling iron. Something large and heavy fell with a crash; the ship's boats on the spar-deck were smashed to bits; burning *débris* fell all round us and we were enveloped in an impenetrable smoke. At the time we did not know what had happened, but afterwards we learned that it was the foremost funnel which had fallen.

The terrified signalmen, losing their presence of mind, huddled together right under the falling spar-deck, and carried us with them in their rush. It took some time before we could compel them to stop and listen to reason.

It was now 2.30 p.m.

When the smoke had somewhat cleared I tried to go to the poop to see what had happened to the after turret, but along the upper deck no communication between bow and stern was possible.

I attempted to pass through the upper battery, whence to the poop the nearest way was through the Admiral's cabin, but here the staff officers' quarters were burning furiously. Turning back, I met Flag Lieutenant Kruijanoffsky on the ladder hurrying downwards.

"Where are you going to?"

"Into the steering compartment; the rudder is disabled," he shouted to me in passing.

"That is all that is wanting," thought I to myself, rushing up on deck.

Quickly going on to the fore-bridge I could not at first get my bearings, because, not far to starboard, our fleet was steaming past, bearing on an opposite course. The *Navarin*,—which ought to have been astern—was now coming up to us, going at full speed and cutting through a big breaker. She especially impressed herself on my memory. It was evident that, owing to our steering gear being out of order, we had turned nearly 16 points.

The line of our fleet was very irregular and the intervals varied, especially in the 3rd squadron. I could not see the leading ships; they were to windward of us and hidden by the smoke of the fires. The enemy was also in the same direction. Taking my bearings by the sun and wind, I should say that our fleet was steering approximately S.E., and the enemy stood to the N.E. of us.

In the event of the flag-ship falling out of the line during the battle, the torpedo-boats *Biedovy* and *Buistry* were immediately to come to her assistance in order to take off the Admiral and staff and put them on board an uninjured ship. But, however much I looked on either side, no torpedo-boats were to be seen. Could we signal? But with what? All means of signalling had long since been destroyed.

Meanwhile, though we were unable to see the enemy on account of the smoke, they had a good view of us, and concentrated their fire on the battered battleship in the hope of sinking us. Shells simply poured upon us—a veritable whirlwind of fire and iron. Lying almost stationary in the water, and slowly working her engines so as to get on the proper course and follow the fleet, the *Suvoroff* offered her battered sides in turn to the enemy, firing wildly from those of her guns which were still serviceable, and, alas! they were few in number. The following is what Japanese eye-witnesses wrote about us:[21]

"On leaving the line the flag-ship, though burning badly, still steamed after the fleet, but under the fire we brought to bear upon her, she rapidly lost her foremast and both funnels, besides being completely enveloped in flames and smoke. She was so battered that scarcely any one would have taken her for a ship, and yet, even in this pitiful condition, like the flag-ship which she was, she never ceased to fire as much as possible with such of her guns as were serviceable."

I will quote another extract from a report on the operations of Admiral Kamimura's squadron:

"The *Suvoroff*, subjected to the fire of both our squadrons, left the line. Her upper part was riddled with holes, and she was entirely enveloped in smoke. Her masts had fallen and her funnels came down one after the other. She was unable to steer, and her fires increased in density every moment. But, even outside the fighting line, she still continued firing, so that our bravest sailors credited her with making a plucky resistance."

And now to return to my personal observations and impressions.

Amidst the rumbling fire of our own guns, the bursting of the enemy's shells, and the roaring of the flames, I was, of course, unable to think about the direction to which we were turning—

whether to or from the wind, but I soon found out. When the battleship, turning on her course, lay stern on to the wind, the smoke from the flames of the burning spar-deck leapt right up to the fore-bridge where I was standing. While occupied in looking for the torpedo-boats, I had probably not noticed the danger creeping towards me, and only realised it on finding myself enveloped in an impenetrable smoke. Burning air parched my face and hands, while a caustic smell of burning almost blinded me. Breathing was impossible. I felt I must save myself, but to do so I had to go through the flames, for there was no other way on to the poop. For a moment the thought flashed across me to jump from the bridge on to the forward 12-inch turret, but to remember where I was, to choose places to which and whence to jump, was impossible. How did I get out of this hell? Perhaps some of the crew who had seen me on the bridge dragged me out! How I arrived on the upper battery on a well-known spot near the ship's ikon, I can't remember, and I can't imagine!

Having recovered my breath, drunk some water and rubbed my eyes, I looked about. It seemed quite pleasant here. The large ikon case was still unbroken, and with the exception of the first shell which had destroyed the temporary dressing station, the quiet of this little corner had apparently been undisturbed. Among some of the crew who were standing by I recognised a few of Demchinsky's signalmen, and, in reply to my enquiries as to his whereabouts, they told me that having been wounded he had made his way to the hospital.

They were standing silently and outwardly were calm, but from the way in which they looked at me I noticed that they were all possessed by some undefined feeling of fear, as well as of expectation and hope. They appeared to believe, or to wish to believe that I was still able to issue the necessary order which would save them, and so they waited. But what order could I give? I might advise them to go below—to take cover under the armoured deck and await their fate, but this they could have done of their own accord. They wanted a different order, for they still felt themselves indispensable to the fight, if it were to be continued. These "tempered" men were just the men we wanted.

And to me, indeed, it seemed useless as well as cruel to shatter their belief—to stamp out the last spark of hope—to tell them the hard truth—to say, in fact, that it was of no use our fighting, and that all was over. No! I couldn't! On the contrary, I was filled with a desire to mislead them—to feed that flame of hope. Rather let them die in the happy consciousness of victory, life, and glory, coming perhaps in a few moments.

As already said, the place where the church was usually rigged[22]—and which the doctor had (so unluckily) selected for his temporary dressing station—had been fairly fortunate, but now, abaft the centre 6-inch turrets, the fire had commenced to make its way. Proceeding thither, we set to work dragging away the burning *débris*, extinguishing it, or throwing it overboard through the huge holes in the ship's side. Finding an undamaged water-main and a piece of a hose (without a nozzle), we worked quietly and in earnest. We extinguished some burning furniture, but alongside it, behind the thin, red-hot, steel partition separating us from the officers' quarters, another fire burst forth, whose roar could at times be heard even amidst the noise of the battle. Occasionally a man fell wounded, and either lay where he was, or got up and walked or crawled to the ladder leading below. No attention was paid to him—What mattered it? one more, one less!

How long we were thus employed—five, ten, or fifteen minutes—I do not know, but suddenly the thought occurred to me, "The conning tower—what is happening there?"

I went up quickly, fatigue and depression at once vanishing. My mind was as clear as possible, and I saw at once that, as the smoke was pouring through the great rents on the port side, the starboard must be the windward side. I proceeded thither. Creeping with difficulty on to the upper deck through the torn hatchway, I scarcely recognised the place where a short time since we had stood with Demchinsky. Movement was literally impossible. Astern, the spar-deck had fallen down and was burning in a bright flame on the deck; in front of me was a heap of *débris*. The ladders to the bridge had gone and the starboard end of the bridge had been destroyed; even the gangway under the bridge on the other side was blocked. I was obliged to go below again and come up on the port side. Here, matters were rather better, as, although fallen and burning, the pieces of the spar-deck were not scattered about in such confusion as on the other side. The 6-inch turret appeared to be still uninjured, and was keeping up a hot fire; the ladder to the bridge was whole, but blocked with burning hammocks, which I at once set five or six men, who were following me, to throw into the water standing on the deck. Suddenly a shell whistled past us, quite close. Everything seemed to start up, and splinters rained upon us. "That must be in the 6-inch turret," thought I to myself, half closing my eyes, and holding my breath so as not to swallow the gas. Sure enough, as the smoke cleared away, only one helpless-looking gun stuck defiantly out of the turret, while out of the armoured door of the latter came its commander, Lieutenant Danchich.

"Mine's done for too; the muzzle of one has been carried away, and the elevating gear of the other is smashed."

Going to the door I looked in. Of the gun's crew two lay huddled up in a curious manner, while one sat motionless, staring with wide-open eyes, holding his wounded side with both hands. A gun captain, with a worried, business-like look, was extinguishing some burning cloths.

"What are you doing here?"

"I want to go to the conning tower."

"Why? There's no one there."

"No one! What do you mean?"

"It's a fact. Bogdanoff has just passed through; he said it was all smashed to pieces—had caught fire, and they'd abandoned it. He went out just as the bridge fell in—right on to me—I wasn't touched—lucky!"

"Where's the Admiral?"

At this moment there was another explosion quite close to me, and something from behind hit me in the right leg. It was not hard, and I felt no pain. I turned round to look, but none of my men were to be seen. Were they killed, or had they gone below?

"Haven't we any stretchers?" I heard Danchich ask anxiously.

"For whom?" I said.

"Why! for you. You're bleeding."

Looking down I saw that my right leg was standing in a pool of blood, but the leg itself felt sound enough.

It was 3 p.m.

"Can you manage to go? Stop—I'll tell off some one to go with you," said Danchich, making what seemed to me an unnecessary fuss.

I was annoyed, and angrily said: "Who wants to be accompanied?" and bravely started to go down the ladder, not realising what had happened. When a small splinter had wounded me in the waist at the beginning of the fight, it had hurt me; but this time I felt nothing.

Later, in the hospital, when carried there on a stretcher, I understood why it is that during a fight one hears neither groans nor shouts. All that comes afterwards. Apparently our feelings have strict limits for receiving external impressions, being even deeply impressed by an absurd sentence. A thing can be so painful that you feel nothing, so terrible that you fear nothing.

Having passed through the upper and lower batteries, I descended to the mess deck (under the armoured one), to the hospital, but I involuntarily went back to the ladder.

The mess deck was full of wounded.[23] They were standing, sitting, lying—some on mattresses put ready beforehand—some on hastily spread tarpaulins—some on stretchers—some just anyhow. Here it was that they first began to feel. The dreadful noise of deep sighs and half-stifled groans was audible in the close, damp air, which smelt of something sour and disgustingly sickly. The electric light seemed scarcely able to penetrate this stench. Ahead somewhere, in white coats stained with red splotches, busy figures were moving about, and towards them all these piles of flesh, clothes, and bones turned, and in their agony dragged themselves, expecting something from them. It seemed as if a cry, motionless, voiceless, but intelligible, a cry which reached to one's very soul, a request for help, for a miracle, for relief from suffering—though at the price of a speedy death—rose up on all sides.

I did not stop to wait my turn, and, not wishing to put myself before others, quickly went up the ladder to the lower battery, where I met the Flag Captain, who had his head bandaged. (He had been wounded in the back of the neck by three splinters.)

On enquiry I learned that at the same time as the steering gear had been injured and the flag-ship had left her place, the Admiral and Vladimirsky were wounded in the head in the conning tower. The latter had gone below to get his wounds dressed, and had been succeeded in command by Bogdanoff, the third lieutenant. The Admiral's orders were to steer after the fleet.

The fore-bridge was struck by numerous projectiles. Splinters of shells, which penetrated in large quantities under the mushroom-shaped roof of the conning tower, had destroyed all the instruments in it, and had broken the compass, but luckily the telegraph to one engine and the voice-tube to the other were still working. The bridge had caught fire, and the hammocks—with which we had proposed to protect ourselves from splinters—as well as the small chart house behind the conning tower, were also burning. The heat became unbearable, and what was worse—the thick smoke prevented our seeing, which, without a compass, made it impossible to keep on in any particular direction. The only thing left for us to do was to steer from the lower fighting position and abandon the conning tower for some place whence one could see. At this time there were in the conning tower the Admiral, the Flag Captain, and the Flag Navigating Officer—all three wounded; Lieutenant Bogdanoff, Sub-Lieutenant Shishkin and one sailor apparently uninjured. Bogdanoff was the first to come out of the tower on the port side of the bridge, and, pluckily pushing aside the burning hammocks, he dashed forward, disappearing into the flames, which were leaping upward. Following after him, the Flag Captain turned to the starboard side of the bridge, but here everything was destroyed; the ladder was gone and there was no road. Only one way remained—below, into the lower fighting position. With difficulty dragging aside the dead bodies which were lying on the deck, they raised the hatch over the armoured tube, and through it let themselves down into the lower fighting position. Rozhdestvensky, although wounded in the head, back and right leg (besides several small splinter wounds), bore himself most cheerfully. From the lower fighting position the Flag Captain proceeded to the hospital, while the Admiral—leaving here Colonel Filipinoffsky (the Flag Navigating Officer), who was slightly wounded, with orders that, in the absence of other instructions, he was to steer on the old course—went off to look for a place from which he could watch the fight.

The upper deck being a mass of burning wreckage, he was unable to pass beyond where the ship's ikon hung in the upper battery. From here he tried to get through to the centre 6-inch turret on the port side, but was unable to, so proceeded to the starboard turret. It was here that he received the wound which caused him so much pain. (A splinter struck his left leg, severing the main nerve and paralysing the ball of the foot.) He was carried into the turret and seated on a box, but he still had sufficient strength at once to ask why the turret was not firing, and to order Kruijanoffsky, who then came up, to find the gun captains, fall in the crews, and open fire. The turret, however, had been damaged and would not turn. Kruijanoffsky, who had just returned from the disabled steering gear, reported that the rudder had been repaired, but that all three communicators with it were cut. Also there were no means of conveying orders from the lower fighting position to the steering gear, as voice-tubes did not exist, the electric indicators were injured, and the telephone refused to work. It became necessary to steer from the lower fighting position, which meant to turn round in circles rather than to go ahead.

The events which I am relating in chronological order, and in the form of a connected narrative were, of course, not recorded in this manner by me, but were told me at different times and by different people. To attempt, however, to give in detail these half-finished sentences, interrupted suddenly by the burst of a shell close by—the jerked-out remarks thrown at one in passing—the separate words accompanied by gestures, more eloquent far than any words—would be impossible and useless. At that moment, when every one's nerves were highly strung, an exclamation or wave of the hand took the place of many words, fully and clearly interpreting the thought which it was desired to express. Put on paper they would be unintelligible.

Time was measured by seconds; and there was no occasion for words.

There was no actual fire in the lower battery as yet; it was coming from above. But through the hatches, torn funnel casings, and shot holes in the middle deck, burning *débris* was falling below, and here and there small fires burst forth. The men, however, set to work, most pluckily rigging up cover for the wireless fighting station with sacks of coal. The trollies with the 12-pounder cartridges which had been collected here (as the ammunition supply rails had been damaged) were in danger of catching fire, so several had to be thrown overboard. However, despite the difficulties in extinguishing the fire, it was at length got under.

Besides spreading in the natural course it was assisted, of course, by the enemy's projectiles, which continued to rain upon us. The losses among the crew still continued to be heavy, and I myself was wounded in the left elbow, as well as being struck by two small splinters in the side.

62

CHAPTER V

I remembered that in the event of the flag-ship leaving the line, the torpedo-boats, *Biedovy* and *Buistry*, were to come to her in order to transfer the Admiral and his staff to another and uninjured ship. In such circumstances, in order to avoid confusion, until the flag had been transferred or until a signal had been made as to the handing over of the command, the fleet was to be led by the ship following the one which had fallen out of the line.

I do not presume to be able to say whether our other ships could see that no torpedo-boats had come up to the *Suvoroff*! Whether they could all see that no signal was possible from the battered, burning battleship, minus funnels and masts! Whether it ought in consequence to have been taken for granted that the command naturally devolved on the next ship according to seniority! and whether she should in some way or another have shown that she had taken over command! In any case the *Alexander* (more correctly, her captain, Bukvostoff) carried out the orders and did her duty. After the flag-ship had fallen out of the line, receiving no fresh instructions, she took the lead and continued the fight.

From the time when I saw the *Alexander* passing close to us on a south-easterly course, she steamed for twenty minutes, gradually inclining to the south in order to prevent the enemy from getting ahead and crossing her T. At the same time the Japanese, elated by their first success, again endeavoured to realise their main idea of a concentrated attack on the leading ship, and so wrapped up were they in this objective that they went ahead too fast, leaving nothing to prevent the *Alexander* passing astern in a north-easterly direction.

She immediately took advantage of this and turned sharp to the north, calculating with luck to fall in force upon their rear and subject them to a raking fire. The Japanese in their reports fix the time of this movement differently; some at 2.40 P.M., others at 2.50 P.M. (the moment of the sinking of the *Oslyabya*, which under the concentrated fire of six of Admiral Kamimura's armoured cruisers had left the line even before the *Suvoroff*). According to my own calculations, the latter time was the more likely to be correct. If the enemy's fleet had turned "in succession," as it had done at the commencement of the battle, this manoeuvre of the *Alexander's* might have been successful, but, realising the gravity of the moment, Togo, on this occasion, gave the order to turn 16 points to port "together." The manoeuvre was not altogether successful. The 1st squadron (*Mikasa, Shikishima, Fuji, Asahi, Kasuga*, and *Nisshin*) performed it correctly, but Kamimura, with his cruisers—probably not having made out the signal and expecting the order to turn "in succession" on to the former course—quickly passed our fleet as well as his own battleships (which were on the opposite course), and masked their fire. He then had plenty of room to turn (he turned "in succession") and, after overtaking the battleships, to form single column line ahead.

For a moment confusion prevailed, for which the Japanese might have paid dearly, but owing to its condition our fleet was unable to reap the advantage. Making full use of their speed, the Japanese not only succeeded in righting their distances, but attained their object, *i.e.* came out across the *Alexander's* course, forcing her to the south.

Through the starboard portholes of our batteries we were now able plainly to see the *Alexander*, which was almost on our beam and steering straight towards us—the remainder following her. The distance rapidly diminished, and with our glasses we could clearly see her battered sides, broken bridges, burning cabins and spar-deck, but her funnels and masts were still standing. After her came the *Borodino*, burning furiously. The enemy had already succeeded in forging ahead, and we now lay between the fleets. Our ships approached from starboard, *i.e.* the port side of the *Suvoroff*, and we came under a hot fire. Our forward 12-inch turret (the only one that was now serviceable) took an active part in the fight, and no attention was paid to falling shells. I was wounded in the left leg, but only looked down with regret at my torn boot! We all waited, holding our breath, watching the Japanese fire, which was apparently concentrated on the *Alexander*. At times she seemed completely enveloped in flames and brown smoke, while round her the sea literally boiled, throwing up great pillars of water. Nearer and nearer she came, till the distance was scarcely 2,000 yards. Then—one after another, we saw a whole series of shells strike her fore-bridge and port 6-inch turret, and turning sharply to starboard she steamed away, having almost reversed her course, while after her went the *Borodino*, *Orel*, and others. The turn was hastily made, being neither "in succession" nor "all together,"[24] and the line ahead formation was not maintained. A deafening clamour resounded in our batteries.

"They've given it up. They are going off. They couldn't do it," I heard on all sides.

These simple folk had, of course, imagined that our fleet was returning to the flag-ship in order to rescue her. Their disenchantment was distressing to witness, but still more was it distressing to realise the true significance of what had happened.

How pitiless is memory!—A scene never to be forgotten came clearly and distinctly before my eyes—just such another scene—the same awful picture. After Prince Utomsky's signal on the 10th August our battleships had steamed north-west in the same disorder and just as hurriedly.

"They couldn't do it!"

And the awful, fatal word, which I had not even dared to think, rang in my brain, and seemed to be written in letters of fire on the smoke, on the battered sides, and even on the pale, confused faces of the crew.

Bogdanoff was standing beside me. I caught his eye, and we understood one another. He commenced to talk of it, but suddenly stopping, looked round, and said in an unnaturally calm voice: "We seem to be heeling over to port."

"Yes—some 8 degrees," I answered, and, pulling out my watch and note-book, jotted down: "*3.25 p.m.—a heavy list to port, and a bad fire in the upper battery.*"

I often afterwards thought: why is it that we hide things from one another and from ourselves? Why did not Bogdanoff express his thoughts aloud? and why was it that I did not dare to write even in my own note-book the cheerless word "*Defeat*"? Perhaps within us there still existed some dim hope of a miracle, of some kind of surprise which would change everything? I do not know.

After the *Alexander* had turned, the enemy's ships also turned 16 points "together," and this time the manoeuvre was successfully performed—so successfully, in fact, that it seemed as if they were merely at drill and not in action.

Steering on an opposite course, they passed under our bows, and from the *Suvoroff* it seemed as if we could almost cut into their column. We inclined to starboard after our fleet. (This was, of course, only imagination, for, not being able to steer by surrounding objects but only by compass in the lower fighting position, we were in reality not moving ahead, but were only turning to starboard and to port; remaining almost in the same place.) In passing close to us, the enemy did not miss his opportunity of concentrating his fire on the obstinate ship which refused to sink, and it was, apparently, now that our last turret, the forward 12-inch, was destroyed. According to Japanese reports their torpedo-boats came up at the same time as their fleet and attacked us unsuccessfully, but I did not see them.

A shell entered the gun port of the fourth (from the bows) 12-pounder gun of the lower battery on the port side, and it was a lucky shot, for in addition to carrying away the gun it penetrated the armoured deck. The water poured into the damaged port, and being unable to run back on account of the list to port, fell through this hole into the mess deck, which was most dangerous.

Bogdanoff was the first to call attention to it, and we at once started to make some kind of an obstacle out of coal sacks, and anything else that was handy, so as to cover the hole and stop the water getting in. I say "we," because the few hands left in the battery could not be brought to obey orders. They huddled in corners in a sort of stupor, and we had almost to drag them out by force, and were obliged to work ourselves to set them an example. We were joined by Flag Torpedo Officer Lieutenant Leontieff and Demchinsky, but the latter could only encourage us with words, as both his wrists were bandaged.

At 3.40 p.m. a cheer broke out in the battery, which was taken up all over the vessel, but we were unable to ascertain what had caused it or whence it had originated. Rumour had it that one of the enemy's ships had been seen to sink; some even said two—not one. Whatever may have been the truth, this cheering had the effect of quickly changing the feeling on board, and the depression from which we had been suffering, both on account of the fire which we had seen poured into the *Alexander*, and because of the departure of the fleet, vanished. Men who had been skulking in corners, deaf to the commands and even requests of their officers, now came running to us asking: "Where could they be of use, and what at?" They even joked and laughed: "Hullo! that's only a 6-inch! No more 'portmanteaus' now!"

Sure enough, since the enemy's main body had steamed off, we had only been subjected to the fire of Admiral Dewa's light cruisers, which, in comparison to what we had been under before, was almost imperceptible.

Commander V. V. Ignatzius had remained below after the second wound in his head had been dressed, and, unable to restrain himself at such a moment, paying no heed to the doctors, he ran up the ladder into the battery, shouting: "Follow me, lads! To the fire—to the fire! we have only got to get it under!"

Various non-combatants in the mess deck (belonging to the hospital), and men who were slightly wounded and had gone down to get their wounds dressed, doubled after him. A chance shot struck the hatchway, and when the smoke cleared away neither ladder, nor Commander, nor men with him, were in existence!

But even this bloody episode did not damp the men's ardour. It was only one in a hundred others.

In the lower battery where, owing to insufficiency of hands, fires momentarily became more numerous, men came, and work went merrily. Of the ship's officers, besides Bogdanoff, there came Lieutenant Vuiruboff, junior torpedo officer, a robust-looking youth, who, in an unbuttoned coat, rushed about everywhere giving the lead, while his shout of "Tackle it! Stick to it!" resounding amongst smoke and flames, gave strength to the workers. Zotoff came for a short time; he was wounded in the left side and arm. Prince Tsereteli looked out from the mess deck, asking how things were going. Kozakevitch was carried past, wounded a second time, and now dangerously. My servant, Matrosoff, appeared and almost dragged me by force to the dressing station. I got rid of him with difficulty, telling him to go at once to my cabin and get me some cigarettes.

"Very good, sir!" he said, going off as he was bid, and we did not meet again.

"To the guns! Torpedo-boats astern! To the guns!" was shouted on deck.

It was easy to say, "To the guns!" but of the twelve 12-pounder guns in the lower battery only one, on the starboard side, was now serviceable, and there was no chance of using it. The torpedo-boats carefully came up from astern (according to the Japanese, this was about 4.20 P.M.), but in the light gun battery aft (behind the ward-room) there was still one uninjured 12-pounder. Maximoff, a volunteer, on whom the command of the battery had devolved after the officers had fallen, opened a hot fire, and the torpedo-boats, seeing that this strange-looking, battered vessel could still show her teeth, steamed off to wait for a more favourable opportunity.

This event suggested to me the idea of noting the means we had with which to protect ourselves against torpedo attack, or, more properly, to what degree of helplessness we had arrived. There were in the lower battery about fifty men of the crew—all of various ratings. Among them, however, were two gun captains. Of the guns, only one was really serviceable, though the gun captains proposed to "repair" another by substituting for its injured parts pieces from the other ten which were quite unserviceable. There was also Maximoff's gun in the stern light gun battery.

Having finished my inspection of the lower battery I went through the upper to the forward light gun battery (not one of the turrets was fit for action), and I was struck with the picture it presented, illustrating, more clearly than I had yet seen, the action of the enemy's projectiles.

There were no fires; everything that could ignite had already been burned. The four 12-pounder guns had been torn off their mountings, and in vain I looked on them for marks of direct hits. None could be seen. The havoc had clearly been caused by the force of the explosion, and not by the impact of the shell. How was this? Neither mines nor pyroxylene were stored in the battery, so the enemy's shells must have exploded with the force of mines.

To my readers, walking about the crippled wreck of a ship like this and inspecting the damage done may appear strange, but it must be remembered that a peculiar, even extraordinary condition of affairs prevailed on board. "So fearful as not to be in the least terrible." To every one it was perfectly clear that all was over. Neither past or future existed. We lived only in the actual moment, and were possessed with an overpowering desire to do something, no matter what.

Having again gone down to the lower battery, I was proceeding to the stern light gun battery, which I wished to inspect, when I met Kursel.

Verner von Kursel, a Courlandian by birth, and a general favourite with every one in the *Suvoroff's* ward-room, had been in the merchant service almost since his cradle, and could speak every language in Europe, though he was equally bad at all of them. When they chaffed him about this in the ward-room he used to say quite seriously: "I think that I'm better at German than any other!"[25] He had seen and been through so much that he never lost his presence of mind, and nothing prevented him meeting his friends with a pleasant smile.

And so now, nodding his head to me in the distance, he cheerily asked:

"Well! How are you passing the time?"

"Badly," I answered.

"Oh! that's it, is it? They don't seem able to hit me yet, but I see that you have been wounded."

"I was."

"Where are you off to?"

"To have a look at the light guns in the stern and get some cigarettes from my cabin; I have smoked all I had."

"To your cabin?" and Kursel grinned. "I have just come from there, I'll go with you."

Indeed, he seemed likely to be a useful companion, as he knew the most sheltered way.

Having got as far as the officers' quarters, I stopped in amazement. Where my cabin and the two adjoining ones had been was an enormous hole! Kursel laughed heartily, thoroughly enjoying his joke, but growing angry I waved my hand and quickly retraced my steps. Kursel overtook me in the battery and offered me a cigar.

The fires in the lower battery had all been got under and, encouraged by this success, we determined to try our luck in the upper battery. Two firemen produced some new half-made hoses; one end of them we fastened to the water-main with wire, and the other we tied to the nozzle. Then, armed with these and using damp sacks to protect us from the flames, we leaned out through the church hatch whence, having succeeded after some little time in putting the fire out which had been burning in the dressing station we were able to go into the upper battery. All hands worked splendidly, and we soon had extinguished the fire in the part assigned to the church. Then another fire started abaft the centre 6-inch turrets—the place which had been selected, on account of its being protected, for putting the cartridge boxes of the 47-millimetre guns taken down from the bridges. Their removal had been well ordered, for no sooner had we set about extinguishing the fire which was now raging near them than they began to explode. Several of the men fell killed and wounded, and great confusion at once ensued.

"It's nothing—it will cease in a moment," said Kursel.

But explosions became more and more frequent. The new hoses were destroyed, one after the other, and then, suddenly, quite close, there was a loud crash, accompanied with the ring of tearing iron. This was not a 6-inch shell, but the "portmanteaus" again. The men became seized with panic, and, listening to nothing and nobody, rushed below.

When we went down into the lower battery, bitterly disappointed at our want of luck just when things seemed beginning to go so well, something (it must have been a splinter of some kind) struck me in the side and I staggered.

"Wounded again?" enquired Kursel, taking his cigar out of his mouth and leaning tenderly over me.

I looked at him and thought: "Ah! if only the whole fleet were composed of men as cool as you are!"

CHAPTER VI

Meanwhile, having turned abruptly away from the *Suvoroff*, our fleet had steamed off, gradually inclining to starboard so as not to give the Japanese a chance of crossing its T, which they evidently were trying to do. The consequence was that both belligerents moved on the arcs of two concentric circles. Ours on the smaller—the Japanese on the larger.

About 4 p.m. it seemed as if fortune for the last time was endeavouring to smile upon us. In the midst of the thick smoke which was pouring from the damaged funnels, from the guns which were in action, and from the fires on board, and which mingled with the mist still lying on the water, the enemy's main force seemed to separate from and lose sight of ours. Japanese reports, of which I have availed myself, comment very briefly and somewhat obscurely on this event. Nothing is clear save that Togo, believing our fleet was somehow breaking through to the north, went thither in search of it. Kamimura being of a different opinion proceeded with his cruisers in a south and south-westerly direction. At least, the above will alone explain the glowing panegyrics which I find in the reports entitled "The Prowess of Admiral Kamimura." If it had not been for this "prowess," possibly the fight would have ended on 27th May, and our fleet would have had time to close up and recover.

Steering on a south and afterwards south-westerly course, Kamimura heard a heavy cannonade proceeding to the west. He accordingly hastened there to find Admiral Kataoka attacking (till now with little success) our cruisers and transports. Kamimura, commencing to take an active part in the fight, then came upon our main body, which, having almost described a circle with a 5-mile diameter, was returning to the spot where the *Alexander* had made her abrupt turn, and round which the *Suvoroff* was so helplessly wandering.

It was about 5 p.m.

I was standing with Kursel in the lower battery smoking and talking of subjects, not in any way connected with the fight, when suddenly we seemed to be in the midst of the fleet, which, devoid of all formation, was moving northwards. Some ships passed to starboard—some to port—the *Borodino*—Captain Serebryanikoff—leading. The *Alexander*, badly battered and with a heavy list—lying so low that the water almost came into the portholes of the lower battery—was still fighting, firing with such of her guns as were serviceable. I did not see her, but was told that the whole of her bows, from the stem to the 12-inch turret, were torn open.

Having closed up to the main body, the cruisers and transports steamed astern and somewhat to port—attacked by detachments of Admiral Kataoko's squadron. (In addition to Kataoko himself, Admirals Dewa, Uriu, and Togo junior were also there.) Kamimura remained further to starboard, *i.e.* to the east—also heading for the north.

"Portmanteaus" were still raining on us. Word had been received from the engine-room that the men were being suffocated and rapidly falling out, as the ventilators were bringing down smoke instead of air; soon there would be no men left to work the engines! Meanwhile, the electric light grew dim, and it was reported from the dynamo engines that steam was scarce.

"Torpedo-boats ahead!"

We rushed to our only gun (the other had been found to be past repair), but it turned out to be the *Buiny*, which happened to be passing us, and was on her own initiative coming alongside the crippled battleship to enquire if she could be of any assistance.

Kruijanoffsky was ordered by the flag-captain, who was standing on the embrasure, to semaphore to her (with his arms) to "take off the Admiral."

I was watching the *Buiny's* movements from the battery, when suddenly the Admiral's messenger, Peter Poochkoff, hastened towards me.

"Please come to the turret, sir! a torpedo-boat has come alongside, but the Admiral won't leave."

I ought to mention here that Rozhdestvensky had not been to the dressing station, and none of us knew how badly he was wounded because, to all enquiries when he was hit, he angrily replied that it was only a trifle. He still remained sitting on the box in the turret, where he had been placed.

At times he would look up to ask how the battle was progressing, and then would again sit silently, with his eyes on the ground. Considering, however, the state the ship was in, what else could he do? His conduct seemed most natural, and it never occurred to us that these questions were merely momentary flashes of energy—short snatches of consciousness.

On the arrival of the torpedo-boat being reported, he pulled himself together, and gave the order to "Collect the staff,"[26] with perfect clearness, but afterwards, he only frowned, and would listen to nothing.

Assisted by Kursel I crept through the open half-port of the lower battery, out on to the starboard embrasure in front of the centre 6-inch turret. I was in need of help, as my right leg had become very painful, and I could only limp on the heel of my left.

The boatswain and some sailors were at work on the embrasure, sweeping overboard the burning *débris* which had fallen from the spar-deck above. Lying off our starboard bow, and some three or four cables distant, was the *Kamchatka*. Kamimura's cruisers were pouring as heavy a fire into her as into us, but she was an easier victim.

The *Buiny* kept close alongside, dancing up and down. Her Captain, Kolomeytseff, shouting through his speaking trumpet, asked: "Have you a boat in which to take off the Admiral? We haven't!" To this the flag Captain and Kruijanoffsky made some reply. I looked at the turret. Its armoured door was damaged and refused to open properly, so that it was very doubtful if anything as big as a man could get through. The Admiral was sitting huddled up, with his eyes on the ground; his head was bandaged in a blood-stained towel.

"Sir, the torpedo-boat is alongside! we must go," I said.

"Call Filipinoffsky," he replied, without moving.

Rozhdestvensky evidently intended to lead the fleet after hoisting his flag on another ship, and therefore wanted to have with him the flag navigating officer, who was responsible for the dead-reckoning and safety of manoeuvres.

"He will be here in a minute; they have gone for him." The Admiral merely shook his head.

I have not laid stress on the fact that before transferring him to another ship it was necessary to try and arrange some means of getting him there.

Kursel, with the boatswain and two or three sailors, had got hold of some half-burned hammocks and rope from the upper battery, and with these had begun to lash together something in the shape of a raft on which to lower the Admiral into the water and put him on board the torpedo-boat. It was risky, but nothing else was to hand.

The raft was ready. Filipinoffsky appeared, and I hurried to the turret.

"Come out, sir! Filipinoffsky is here."

Rozhdestvensky gazed at us, shaking his head, and not uttering a syllable.

"I don't want to. No."

We were at a loss how to proceed.

"What are you staring at?" suddenly said Kursel. "Carry him; can't you see he is badly wounded?"

It seemed as if it was only for these words and the impulse they supplied for which we were waiting. There was a hum of voices and much bustling about. Some forcing their way into the turret, took hold of the Admiral by his arms and raised him up, but no sooner had he put his left leg to the ground than he groaned and completely lost consciousness. It was the best thing that could have happened.

"Bring him along! Bring him along! Splendid! Easy now! the devil! Take him along the side! Get to the side, can't you? Stop—something's cracking! What? his coat is being torn! Carry him along!" were the anxious shouts one heard on all sides. Having taken off the Admiral's coat, they dragged him with the greatest difficulty through the narrow opening of the jammed door out on to the after embrasure, and were just proceeding to fasten him to the raft, when Kolomeytseff did, what a man does only once in his life, and then when inspired. My readers who are landsmen will not realise all the danger of what we were to attempt, but sailors will easily understand the risk. Kolomeytseff brought his vessel alongside and to windward of the mutilated battleship, out of whose battered gun ports stuck her crippled guns, and from whose side projected the broken booms of her torpedo-nets.[27] Dancing up and down on the waves the torpedo-boat at one moment rose till her deck was almost on a level with the embrasure, then rapidly sank away below; next moment she was carried away, and then again was seen struggling towards us, being momentarily in danger of staving in her thin side against one of the many projections from this motionless mass.

The Admiral was carried hurriedly from the after to the bow embrasure, along the narrow gangway between the turrets and the battered side of the upper battery. From here, off the backs of the men who were standing by the open half-port, holding on to the side, he was lowered down, almost thrown, on board the torpedo-boat, at a moment when she rose on a wave and swung towards us.[28]

"Hurrah! the Admiral is on board!" shouted Kursel, waving his cap.

"Hurrah!" cheered every one.

How I, with my wounded legs, boarded her, I don't remember. I can only recollect that, lying on the hot engine-room hatch between the funnels, I gazed at the *Suvoroff*, unable to take my eyes off her. It was one of those moments which are indelibly impressed upon the mind.

Our position alongside the *Suvoroff* was extremely dangerous, as, besides the risk of being crushed, we might, at any moment, have been sunk by a shell, for the Japanese still poured in a hot fire upon both the flag-ship and the *Kamchatka*. Several of the *Buiny's* crew had already been killed and wounded with splinters, and a lucky shot might at any moment send us to the bottom.

"Push off quickly!" shouted Kursel from the embrasure.

"Push off—push off—don't waste a moment—don't drown the Admiral!" bawled Bogdanoff, leaning over the side and shaking his fist at our captain.

"Push off—push off!" repeated the crew, looking out of the battery ports and waving their caps.

Choosing a moment when she was clear of the side, Kolomeytseff gave the order "Full speed astern."

Farewell shouts reached us from the *Suvoroff*. I say from the "*Suvoroff*," but who would have recognised the, till recently, formidable battleship in this crippled mass, which was now enveloped in smoke and flames?

Her mainmast was cut in half. Her foremast and both funnels had been completely carried away, while her high bridges and galleries had been rent in pieces, and instead of them shapeless piles of distorted iron were heaped upon the deck. She had a heavy list to port, and, in consequence of it, we could see the hull under the water-line on her starboard side reddening the surface of the water, while great tongues of fire were leaping out of numerous rents.

We rapidly steamed away, followed by a brisk fire from those of the enemy's ships which had noticed our movements.

It was 5.30 p.m.

As I have previously remarked, up to the last moment in the *Suvoroff* we none of us were aware of the nature of the Admiral's wounds, and, therefore, the immediate question on board the *Buiny* was, which ship was he to board in order to continue in command of the fleet? When, however, the surgeon, Peter Kudinoff, came to render first aid, we at once learned of how the matter lay, for Kudinoff declared that his life was in danger; that he was suffering from fracture of the skull—a portion of it having entered his brain—and that any jolt might have fatal results. Taking into consideration the condition of the weather—a fresh breeze and a fairly heavy swell—he said it would be impossible to transfer him to another ship. Moreover, he was unable to stand, and his general condition, loss of power and memory, wandering, and short flashes of consciousness, rendered him incapable of any action.

From the *Buiny's* engine-room hatch, on which I had chanced to take up my position on going aboard, I proceeded to the bridge, but found that I was not able to stand here because of the rolling, and could only lie. However, while lying down, I was so in the way of those on duty that the Commander advised me in as nice a way as possible to go elsewhere—to the hospital.

We were now overtaking the fleet, and the flag Captain decided that before making any signal, we must in spite of above consult the Admiral, and this was entrusted to me. Picking my way astern with great difficulty, I went down the ladder and looked into the Captain's cabin. The surgeon had finished dressing the Admiral's wounds, and the latter was lying motionless in a hammock with half-closed eyes. But he was still conscious.

On my asking him if he felt strong enough to continue in command, and what ship he wished to board, he turned towards me with an effort, and for a while seemed trying to remember something.

"No—where am I? You can see—command—Nebogatoff," he muttered indistinctly, and then, with a sudden burst of energy, added, "Keep on Vladivostok—course N.23°E.," and again relapsed into a stupor.

Having sent his reply to the flag Captain (I don't remember by whom, but I think it was by Leontieff) I intended to remain in the ward-room, but there was no room. All the cabins and even the upper deck were full of men, as, before coming to the *Suvoroff*, the *Buiny* had picked up over 200 men at the spot where the *Oslyabya* sank. Amongst them were wounded sailors who had been swimming about in the salt water, and others who, when taken up, had been half drowned. The latter, contracted with cramp, and racked with tormenting coughs and pains in their chests, seemed with their bluish faces to be in a worse plight than the most badly wounded.

Passing on to the upper deck I seated myself on a box by the ladder to the officers' quarters.

Signals were fluttering from our mast and orders were being given by semaphore to the torpedo-boats, *Bezuprechny* and *Biedovy*, which were now close up to us.[29] We had already caught up the fleet and were steaming, together with the transports, which were covered, ahead and to starboard, by our cruisers. Still further to starboard, and some 30 cables off, was our main force. The *Borodino* was leading, and after her came the *Orel*; but the *Alexander* was nowhere to be seen.[30] In the distance, still further off, could dimly be made out in the dusk, which was now rapidly creeping on, the silhouettes of the Japanese ships—steaming parallel to us. The flashes of their guns twinkled incessantly along the line, but the stubborn fight was not yet at an end!

Alongside of me I recognised an officer of the *Oslyabya*, and asked him what had actually caused his ship to sink?

Waving his arm in a helpless sort of way, and in a voice full of disgust, he jerked out: "How? it's not very pleasant to remember. Absolutely no luck, that's what sunk her. Nothing but bad luck! They shot straight enough—but it wasn't shooting. It wasn't skill either. It was luck—infernal luck! Three shells, one after the other, almost in the same identical spot—Imagine it! All of them in the same place! All on the water-line under the forward turret! Not a hole—but a regular gateway! Three of them penetrated her together. She almost heeled over at once—then settled under the water. A tremendous rush of water and the partitions were naturally useless. The devil himself couldn't have done anything!"

he hysterically exclaimed, and, covering his face with his hands, went on deck.

About 7 p.m. the enemy's torpedo-boats appeared across the course on which our main force was steering, but rapidly drew off as our cruisers opened fire on them.

"Perhaps they've laid mines!" I thought to myself, and turned on my box, trying to make myself more easy.

"The *Borodino*! Look! the *Borodino*!" was shouted on all sides.

I raised myself, as quickly as possible on my arm, but where the *Borodino* had been nothing was visible save a patch of white foam!

It was 7.10 p.m.

The enemy's fleet having turned sharply to starboard, bore off to the east, and in its place was a group of torpedo-boats, which now surrounded us in a semicircle from the north, east, and west. Preparing to receive their attacks from astern, our cruisers, and we after them, gradually inclined to port,—and then bore almost direct to the west—straight towards the red sky. (There was no compass near me.)

At 7.40 p.m. I still was able to see our battleships, steaming astern of us devoid of formation, and defending themselves from the approaching torpedo-boats by firing. *This was my last note.*

Feeling weak from loss of blood and from the inflammation of my wounds, which were dirty and had not been bandaged, I began to shiver. My head swam, and I went below to get help.

And what of the *Suvoroff?* This is how a Japanese report describes her last moments:

"In the dusk, when our cruisers were driving the enemy northwards, they came upon the *Suvoroff* alone, at some distance from the fight, heeling over badly and enveloped in flames and smoke. The division (Captain-Lieutenant Fudzimoto) of torpedo-boats, which was with our cruisers, was at once sent to attack her. Although much burned and still on fire—although she had been subjected to so many attacks, having been fired at by all the fleet (in the full sense of the word)—although she had only one serviceable gun—she still opened fire, showing her determination to defend herself to the last moment of her existence—so long, in fact, as she remained above water. At length, about 7 P.M., after our torpedo-boats had twice attacked her, she went to the bottom."

In memory of the Suvoroff!

COMPOSITION OF THE OPPOSING FLEETS.

RUSSIAN.

1st Armoured Squadron.

Knyaz Suvoroff. (*Flag.*)

Imperator Alexander.

Borodino.

Orel.

2nd Armoured Squadron.

Oslyabya.

Sissoy Veliki.

Navarin.

Admiral Nakhimoff.

JAPANESE.

1st Squadron.

Mikasa. (*Flag.*)

Shikishima.

Fuji.

Asahi.

Kasuga.

Nisshin.

2nd Squadron.

Idzumo.

Yakumo.

Asama.

Adzuma.

Tokiwa.

Iwatc.

3rd Armoured Squadron.

Imperator Nicolay.

Admiral Senyavin.

Admiral Apraxin.

Admiral Ushakoff.

CRUISERS

Cruiser Squadron.

Oleg.

Aurora.

Dmitri Donskoy.

Vladimir Monomakh.

3rd Squadron.

1st Division.

Itsukushima.

Matsushima.

Hasidate.

Chin Yen.

2nd Division.

Suma.

Chiyoda.

Idzumi.

Akitsushu.

3rd Division.

Kasagi

Chitose.

Otawa.

Niitaka.

4th Division.

Naniwa.

Takachiho.

Tsushima.

Scout Division.

Svietlana.

Akashi.

AUXILIARY CRUISERS.

Almaz.

16 Cruisers.

Ural.

CRUISERS DETAILED FOR CO-OPERATION WITH TORPEDO-BOATS.

Zemtchug.

Izumrud.

Toyohashi.

Maya.

Takao.

Chihaya.

Tatsuta.

Uji.

Yaeyama.

Chokai.

Yamato.

Tsukushi.

DESTROYERS AND TORPEDO-BOATS.

9 Destroyers.

25 Destroyers.

12 Torpedo-Boats, 1st Class.

55 Torpedo-Boats, 2nd Class.

18 Torpedo-Boats, 3rd Class.

FOOTNOTES

[1] These cruisers had no armour protection for their guns.

[2] All, except the naval transports carrying war stores, were left at Shanghai.—A.B.L.

[3] Evidently the *Oslyabya* was omitted by a printer's error. She should come in as the fifth ship, *i.e.* after the *Orel*, and leading the 2nd armoured squadron.—A.B.L.

[4] Cruel irony! We were attempting to force our way through to our *base*, and had been ordered to take with us, if possible, everything in the way of materials and supplies that we might require, so as not to overtax it. The railway was only able with difficulty to supply the army, and we were under no circumstances to count upon its help.

[5] "Together" has a literal meaning: the ships all change direction simultaneously to the same side and at the same angle. By doing this they take up a new formation, parallel to their former line, and to starboard or to port of it, moving ahead or not according to the size of the angle of turning. Shortly after changing direction the order is again given to turn "together" at the same angle, but to the opposite side, and the ships thus find themselves once more in single column line ahead, but at some distance to starboard or to port of their original course.

"Together" is the direct opposite to "in succession," when each ship changes direction as she comes to the spot in which the leading ship has turned—*i.e.* follows her.

<u>6</u> "Samotopy" literally "self-sinkers."—A.B.L.

<u>7</u> Admiral Nebogatoff, with the 3rd squadron, joined the main fleet on 9th May.—A.B.L.

<u>8</u> A play upon the words. The Russian translation of "presentiment" is "feeling before."—A.B.L.

<u>9</u> Fate had not been kind to us. The *Terek* and *Kuban* met no one all the time that they were there, and no one knew of their presence in those waters.

<u>10</u> Verbatim in the context.—A.B.L.

<u>11</u> According to Japanese reports, Togo, who was stationed with his main body somewhere off Fusan, was at this time in complete ignorance of our whereabouts and was waiting for news from both north and south.

<u>12</u> A point = 11¼°.

<u>13</u> At Port Arthur the long Japanese shells of big calibre guns were nicknamed ("chemodani") "portmanteaus." Indeed, what else could you call a shell, a foot in diameter and more than 4 feet long, filled with explosive?

<u>14</u> A flag-sub-lieutenant.

<u>15</u> Japanese officers said that after Port Arthur had capitulated, while waiting for the Baltic fleet, they worked up to their high state of preparation as follows:—At target practice every gun

captain fired five live shells out of his gun. New guns were afterwards substituted for those worn out.

<u>16</u> According to thoroughly trustworthy reports, the Japanese in the battle of Tsu-shima were the first to employ a new kind of explosive in their shells, the secret of which they bought during the war from its inventor, a colonel in one of the South American Republics. It was said that these shells could only be used in guns of large calibre in the armoured squadrons, and that is how those of our ships engaged with Admiral Kataoka's squadron did not suffer the same amount of damage, or have so many fires, as the ships engaged with the battleships and armoured cruisers. Very convincing proofs of this were the cases of the *Svietlana* and *Donskoy*. On 28th May the former was subjected to the fire of two light cruisers, and the latter to the fire of five. In the first place, both were able to hold out for a considerable time, and in the second (and this is most important), they did not catch fire, although on both ships—the *Donskoy*, which was one of the older type, and the *Svietlana*, which was like a yacht— there was considerably more combustible material than on the newer type of battleship.

For a great many years in naval gunnery two distinct ideas have prevailed—one is to inflict on the enemy, although not necessarily much (in quantity), severe and heavy damage—*i.e.* to stop movement—to penetrate under the water-line—to get a burst in the hull below the water-line—briefly, to put the ship at once out of action. The other is to pour upon him the greatest volume of fire in the shortest time—though it be above water and the actual damage caused by each individual shot be immaterial—in the hope of paralysing the ship, trusting that if this were done it would not be difficult to destroy her completely—that she would, in fact, sink by herself.

With modern guns, in order to secure the first of the above ideas, solid armour-penetrating projectiles must be employed—*i.e.* thick-coated shells (whose internal capacity and bursting charge is consequently diminished), and percussion fuzes with retarded action, bursting the shell inside the target. To secure the second idea shells need only be sufficiently solid to ensure their not bursting at the moment of being fired. The thickness of their walls may be reduced to the minimum, and their internal capacity and bursting charge increased to the utmost limits. The percussion fuzes should be sensitive enough to detonate at the slightest touch.

The first of the above views prevails chiefly in France, the second in England. In the late war we held the first, and the Japanese the second.

[17] A colonel of the marine artillery—flag gunnery officer.

[18] By the Admiral's order the iron oil drums, instead of being thrown away, had been converted into buckets, and these home-made contrivances were placed about the decks.

[19] In the Battle of Tsu-shima the Japanese losses were:

Killed   113

Dangerously wounded   139

Severely wounded   243

Slightly wounded   42

These figures are sufficiently eloquent, even allowing for the reports of Japanese officers to be somewhat partial. Almost half of the casualties (252 out of 537) were killed and dangerously wounded, the other half were severely and slightly wounded—less than 8 per cent. The total number was insignificant. Our shells evidently either never burst, or burst badly, *i.e.* in a few large pieces. The Japanese bursting charge was seven times stronger than ours, and consisted not of pyroxylene, but of shimose (and perhaps of something still more powerful). Shimose, on exploding, raises the temperature one and a half times higher than pyroxylene. In fact, one might say that a Japanese shell bursting well did as much damage as twelve of ours bursting equally well. And this ours rarely succeeded in doing!

<u>20</u> The ships nearest to us reported afterwards that the armoured shield on our after turret had been blown right up above the bridges, and then was seen to fall crumpled up on to the poop. What had actually happened was not known.

<u>21</u> In order to establish a connection between the facts which I personally saw and noted down, and in order to be able to explain the Japanese movements, I shall have recourse to sources which can hardly be suspected of partiality towards us. I refer to two Japanese official publications which are both entitled "Nippon-Kai Tai-Kai-Sen" ("The Great Battle in the Sea of Japan"). The books are illustrated by a number of photographs and plans taken at different moments of the fight, and contain the reports of various ships and detachments. A few quite immaterial differences in description of detail by various witnesses have not been removed, as they only give the stamp of truth to the publication.

I must request my readers to excuse the heavy, and at times incoherent language introduced by me in these quotations. The reason for this is my wish to keep as near as possible to the original, and, in the construction of its sentences, Japanese is totally different to any European language.

<u>22</u> In a ship there is no proper church compartment. The church is only rigged when a service is to be held.

<u>23</u> There were probably more here than in the whole of the Japanese fleet.

<u>24</u> Whether this turn was intentional or accidental, owing to the damage done to her steering communicators, will for ever remain a secret.

<u>25</u> Courland is one of the Baltic Provinces where German is spoken.—A.B.L.

<u>26</u> Of all the wounded members of the staff, who were below, under the armoured deck, it was only possible to "collect" two—Filipinoffsky and Leontieff. The former was in the lower fighting position, which was hermetically separated from the mess deck, and received a current of fresh air through the armoured tube of the conning tower. (All the same he had to sit by candle light, as the lamps had gone out.) The latter was at the exit hatch. The mess deck was in darkness (the electric light had gone out) and was full of suffocating smoke. Hurrying along to find the staff, we called them by name; but received no answers. The silence of the dead reigned in that smoky darkness, and it is probable that all who were in the closed compartments under the armoured deck, where

the ventilators took smoke instead of air, gradually becoming suffocated, lost consciousness and died. The engines had ceased to work. The electric light had given out for want of steam; and no one came up from below. Of the 900 men composing the complement of the *Suvoroff*, it would not be far wrong to say that, at this time there remained alive only those few who were gathered together in the lower battery and on the windward embrasure.

[27] It was impossible to come up on the leeward side, because of the smoke and flames.

[28] He was transferred to the *Biedovy* on the morning of 28th May.—A.B.L.

[29] The *Bezuprechny* was ordered to go to the *Nicolay* and to give (by semaphore) the late commander's instructions to the new, *i.e.* Nebogatoff. The *Biedovy* was sent to the *Suvoroff* to take off the remainder of her complement, but the flag-ship could not be found.

[30] She had gone down about 5.30 P.M.

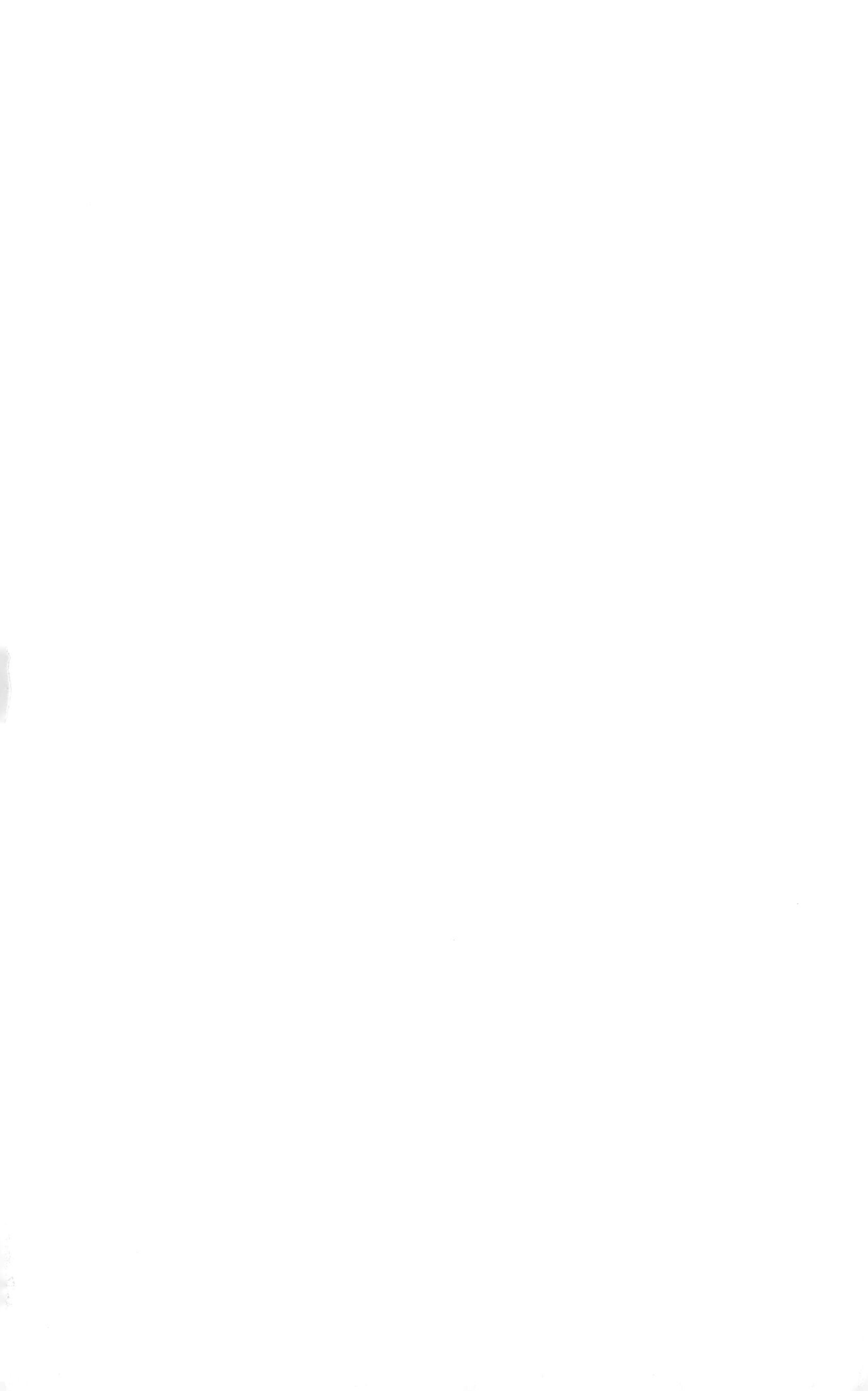